Rent as Public Revenue: Issues and Methods

Rent as Public Revenue: Issues and Methods

Robert Schalkenbach Foundation
Henry George Institute

Rent as Public Revenue: Issues and Methods

Edited and designed by Lindy Davies

isbn   978-0-9905043-3-7

Library of Congress Control Number 2017964563

Contents

Introduction: The COLT Project

by Gilbert Herman

In 1968 Bob Clancy, who was Director of the Henry George School in New York City at that time, conceived of the idea to create a manual that would explain the practical application of George's ideas. He felt there lacked a comprehensive guide that would assist Georgists in demonstrating how the theory can be put into real world implementation and also show non-Georgists how practical his theory is. Also, many Georgists at that time were not aware of the relevance of George's ideas to broader applications of land value taxation to special uses — air rights, franchises, easements and the electromagnetic spectrum.

Bob devised the acronym COLT to stand for two meanings. The first and obvious one was the Committee On Land Taxation. The other meaning was that COLT would be just a start on developing a comprehensive guide to the practical implementation of LVT – just as a colt develops into an adult horse, so this committee would grow into a wider effort to expand the information contained in this beginning guide.

The committee was informal and part-time. I was honored to be a participant in this effort. The work entailed a lot of research, reading and learning about some topics that were new to all of us. None of us were experts in the topics we wrote about. The Internet didn't exist and we relied on books, journals, magazines, newspapers, encyclopedias (remember them?) and files that the school had. The school had great collections of this material in its library — which Bob had played a key role in amassing.

There were only four "members" of this committee. Bob

Clancy, of course, was the guiding force behind it. Peter Patsakos worked for the school — I believe he managed the International Division — and also taught courses. (Unfortunately, he has since passed away). Charles Leonard was a medical student and a student at HGS and did the bulk of the work. I was working at the time in private industry.

Unfortunately, Bob's vision of an expanded COLT never materialized. So I am pleased that this effort is being undertaken today — especially in the difficult and contentious times we live in now, when these ideas are more needed than ever. Bob would certainly be overjoyed.

EDITOR'S NOTE: Special thanks are due to Carl Shaw, who got this project started by hiring a typist to digitize the entire 1971 COLT manual, which will be made available online.

NOTE ON DOCUMENTATION: Aiming to maximize readability, I have chosen to eschew inline citations. Sources mentioned in the text or in footnotes are listed, alphabetically by author (or organization) in the Works Cited. — L. D.

Preface: Rent As Revenue

by Lindy Davies

I n the late 1960s a group of alumni of the Henry George School of New York, led by the school's Director, Robert Clancy, set out to "gather together relevant material on ways and means of putting land value taxation into practice." The group envisioned the publication as the first in what would ideally become a continually-updated annual series. There was need for such an effort: over the years the Henry George Schools had acquainted many thousands of students with the principles of Georgist political economy, but there were precious few "on the ground" campaigns. The COLT group believed that a broad, factual discussion of *how it can be done* would stimulate efforts to *get it done* in real jurisdictions. But, alas, support for the Committee's activities evaporated, and the only version of the manual that ever appeared was the limited, mimeographed edition.

There is still a need for this work. Its audience is more important than it is large (but it will likely continue to grow). This anthology's goal is not to make the case for the Georgist remedy. We assume that readers already understand the basic ideas of Georgist political economy, and we endeavor to explain how that remedy can be applied in the real world.

We start by assuming that the rent of land is the natural source of revenue for the community's needs. We also start by assuming that "broad-based tax policy" is fundamentally misguided, because taxation that falls on the production of goods and services imposes unnecessary, unjust deadweight losses on society. Readers who wish to know more about these ideas have not far to search: the Henry

George Institute offers a a free, introductory online course at its website (www.henrygeorge.org).

Over the years since 1970 it became evident that the term "land value taxation" is less than ideal. Some argued (correctly in theory) that the public collection of land rent isn't "taxation" at all, but simply the community's recovery of a value that the community itself has created. Others noted that "land" is not an opportune term with which to make our case — calling to mind, as it does, bucolic vistas of valleys and hills, far removed from today's complex economic problems. In literal terms, this isn't a problem; we can recall that Henry George defined "economic land" not as the mere surface of the earth, but rather as "the entire material universe, except for human beings and their products." We hasten to remind folks that the most valuable natural resource in any modern economy is not water, oil fields or diamond mines, but the ground under the center of any great city, which is often worth many thousands of dollars per square foot.

Nevertheless, because land — the set of all natural opportunities — encompasses more than many people realize, it seems clear that a more inclusive term like "natural resources" works better. And, when we're talking about the income that society ought to gain from allowing exclusive access to these natural resources, it seems a good idea to call it what it is: rent. Hence the title of this volume.

What, then, is rent?

This is often made to seem more complicated than it really is. Of course, the conversational sense of "rent" as in when one rents a car, or rents an apartment, differs from the precise economic sense. Following from the classical economists, Henry George defined "economic rent" as the share of aggregate wealth that is taken by the owners of land — the economic factor that is fixed in supply, and not produced by human labor. This is primarily a term of political economy, which focuses on the "wealth of nations" — aggregate, society-wide production and distribution. Mainstream Economics texts tend to define "economic rent" in a way that seems quite different at first glance, but in fact is not so different at all. The standard definition is "Any payment to a factor of production in excess of the cost needed to bring that factor into production."

Thus, economic rent is a pure surplus. Since land is not produced and has no cost of production, all the income it generates is economic rent.

To be sure, there are other forms of unearned income. Income attributable to patents or to exclusive licenses is a privilege granted by government, not created by the recipients. Subsidies, of course, are unearned, as are payments attributable to graft or corruption. It can even be argued that pay increases enjoyed by members of labor unions, or even minimum-wage recipients, are unearned, to the extent that they are surpluses above market wage for that form of labor.

However, Georgists argue that all such privileges are fundamentally different from the rent of land, for a simple reason. They are all granted, in some way or other, by society, and they can all be taken away by society. Production can go on without them. However, production cannot go on without land; access to natural opportunities is a requirement of any form of production. Henry George referred to those various non-land monopolies as "lesser robbers." If they were all removed, society's wealth-producers would be beset with a strengthened land monopoly, "the robber that takes all that is left."

That is why, when we refer to "rent as revenue," we insist on *the rent of natural resources and opportunites*. Other forms of monopoly can be dealt with through other reforms; we are concerned with "the robber that takes all that is left."

Implementing the Georgist Remedy: Loads of Challenges

by Lindy Davies

Many readers finish Henry George's classic *Progress and Poverty* and start rubbing their hands, eager to get to work. The book offers a compelling vision that combines justice (equity) and freedom (efficiency). At first glance, the path to implementing Henry George's remedy seems clear. His statement "We must make land common property" frightened people when taken out of context, but George immediately offered a practical means for achieving that end. His proposal emphasized practicality. While it would be morally acceptable, he said, for the state to take possession of the land, and let it out to those who wish to use it, doing so would create huge disruption. "It is not necessary to confiscate land," George wrote, "it is only necessary to confiscate rent." Secure land tenure must be preserved, because owners have an inalienable right to their improvements to the land, wealth they have created with their own labor. George's remedy was designed to secure these two equally vital fundamental rights.

Henry George thought the transition to the optimum public revenue system would be easy, as soon as enough people came to understand its importance. Property taxes were a major source of revenue in George's day. Though they are less of a factor today, they are still a significant source of local revenue (and are, alas, more popular with economists than with voters). George advised that "We already take some rent in taxation. We have only to make some changes in our modes of taxation to take it all." Georgists have long followed this advice, advocating property tax reform in which tax rates on land are gradually increased, while those on buildings (and later, ideally, on labor and all forms of capital) are decreased.

This has been done, in a number of places, and it has achieved the positive results predicted for it — albeit modestly, and subject to several qualifications. Its application has been limited, and assessment of its effects have been muddled by many complicating factors. Without a doubt, however, wherever land value taxation has been tried, it has tended to increase new construction. Yet it has not caught on — and that seems mysterious, given the reform's demonstrable advantages. Revenue raised via land value taxation need *not* be raised from taxes that make building riskier, prices higher, labor more expensive and commerce less profitable.

Though many argue that there would be no *economic* downside to doing so, land value taxation needn't be imposed all at once. Barring extraordinary circumstances, a gradual strategy seems to be the only feasible one. George's recommendation to utilize the existing property tax system can still be a workable starting point. In most cities, homeowners tend to have a high ratio of building value to land value. This means that a transition to a two-rate property tax system (usually designed to be revenue-neutral at first) can be done in such as way that the majority of voters will pay less property tax. For example, the 1997 campaign to adopt two-rate property taxation in Allentown, Pennsylvania used this strategy explicitly. While land-intensive businesses such as car dealerships and big-box stores screamed their opposition, volunteers manned phone banks to inform individual homeowners that LVT would save them money. It worked; Allentown not only has a two-rate property tax to this day, it has since increased the ratio of land tax to building tax — five times.

It is a settled matter of economic theory that a city's investments in public infrastructure and services create at least enough land rent to cover their costs. Therefore the rent of a city's land would suffice as a tax base; no other municipal taxes would be needed (this is known as the "Henry George Theorem").* It isn't hard to

---

* This theorem had notably been articulated by Nobelists William Vickrey and Joseph Stiglitz. It was initially suggested by Gilbert Tucker in his 1946 book *The Self-Supporting City*. This book was reprinted in 2010 by the Robert Schalkenbach Foundation, with an afterword by William Batt that surveyed the current literature on the HGT.

imagine how a city's economy would improve, were it to remove the tax burdens it imposes on wages, sales, housing and commercial buildings. Conceptually, these are not difficult arguments to make. In practice, land value taxation works as predicted, where it has been applied, to a degree sufficient to lift its economic benefits above the noise of other factors. It's a great idea. It works. Why, then, has it not made more progress?

We'll consider five major reasons for land value taxation's heretofore lack of traction, and then briefly discuss mitigation strategies (subsequent chapters will deal with these issues in depth).

I. Public ignorance and indifference

Activists tend, of course, to believe that the issue they are moved to work for is very important. Because of the economic and moral primacy of the land question, Georgists tend to see their cause as *the* issue. Rhetorically, this puts them in a difficult position. They must make their case to people who have never even thought about land as a public revenue source — or who have been taught that land's role is insignificant. The property tax is most commonly a local tax, a tax among other taxes. Taxation at state and federal levels often takes a bigger bite. This is not to say that property taxation isn't controversial. It engenders strong resistance, especially in sprawling suburban areas, and it is thought to be regressive, as sudden increases in assessments on low- and fixed-income property owners are seen as highly unfair. This means that when property taxation does make the news, it almost always seen in a negative light.

In general, taxation is seen as an inevitable penalty on doing business — or in the words of Oliver Wendell Holmes, "the price we pay for a civilized society." Discussions of tax policy tend to revolve around the question of the *amount* of taxation: liberals want a larger public sector, a stronger and better-provisioned government; conservatives want people to enjoy more of their hard-won wages and profits. For Georgists, the *amount* of public revenue is less important than the *source* — but in conventional tax policy the source of public revenue is simply a matter of practical politics. Since taxation is, in its nature, a penalty on production, "broad-based" tax policy is favored, to spread the burden among as many different sources as can be found. From the Georgist perspective, taxes which fall on production — on wages, sales, imports, buildings, etc. — are economically no more than what Henry George calls the "lesser robbers." * Eliminating these burdens on labor and capital would simply leave more to be collected in rent by the landowners. This means that any conversation about the fairness and efficiency of land value taxation must, to a large extent, be about tax policy in general. Thus, the conversation is framed in the very terms that the logic of land value taxation transcends. Indeed, many Georgists are eager to point out that the "land value tax" is not actually a tax. This is certainly true, if by "tax" we mean a charge that burdens production and distorts economic decision-making. The collection of land rent for public revenue places no burden on production, and is, at worst, economically neutral; it is only a "tax" in the sense that it is source of public revenue.

Land ownership is a prized investment, an important source of economic security. Tax policy often favors it, and home equity gives middle-class people access to liquidity that they couldn't get in any other way. Furthermore, many people have little or no savings; they look to the appreciated value of their real estate to provide them with a nest egg. Because taxation is seen as a sort of "social dues," most people are willing to accept taxes on their income, or built into the prices of things they buy. They are wary, however, of any proposal that might diminish the value of their real estate. Thus middle-class homeowners make common cause with poor folks who have no asset but their land — creating a strong bloc against property taxes in general. They might see a tax on land as an even more pernicious kind of property tax.

2. Perceived inadequacy as a revenue base

The role of land in the property tax base is not clearly understood — and it is often de-emphasized. "Housing" is the common euphemism for "real estate," but the volatile element in the "housing" market is the price of land, not of buildings. Furthermore, the value of commercial and income-producing buildings is depreciable for income tax purposes, which creates a persistent incentive for public assessors to overvalue buildings,

* In *Protection or Free Trade*, 1886, chapter 25.

relative to land. This is the path of least resistance for assessors (because land and buildings are commonly taxed at the same rate, the error seems inconsequential), yet it lends support to the common view that urban land is not an important economic factor.

This perception is abetted by mainstream academic economics. Mason Gaffney and others have persuasively argued that eliminating consideration of land as a separate factor of production was a major goal in the development of neoclassical economics. This did not confer any analytical benefits; indeed, analysis of economic cycles which explicitly factors in the influence of land has solved riddles that have defied mainstream economists.[†] Be that as it may, however, college "econ" courses usually mention that land *was* considered a factor of production by the classical economists — but assure their students that land's influence has diminished over time. They reinforce this by using a question-begging "economic" definition of land as restricted to the original, pre-development fertility of the soil. The value of location, and of the presence and contributions of the community, are not considered to be part of land!

In *The Corruption of Economics* (1994), Mason Gaffney implies that there was an ideological purpose behind the initial formulation of neoclassical economics. Henry George argued that the private ownership of land is at the base of systemic economic dysfunction in modern society. Yet, the private ownership of land and natural opportunities was the key to the Great American Fortunes that endowed the economics departments of major universities. Whether or not it was fully intentional, one legacy of the "neoclassical revolution" is the widely-held belief that land rent amounts to a very small part of the aggregate income of a modern economy; the figure of 2-3% is often cited. This is demonstrably untrue; people who own, and deal in, real estate understand it to be nonsense — but it nevertheless serves as a starting point for many considerations of economics and public policy.

This leads to a state of affairs in which the role of land in myriad economic concerns — banking and finance, public revenue, corporate assets, economic cycles, national saving and spending, etc. — is thought to be utterly sacrosanct and, indeed, inextricable.

---

† Authors Fred Harrison and Fred Foldvary, employing Georgist analysis, successfully predicted the last two major recessions, well in advance.

This is circular reasoning that spins at high RPM: there's no point in considering land's distinct economic role, because it is not considered to *have* any distinct economic role.

3. Land assessment assumed to be too difficult

People generally think of "assessment" as an attempt to estimate the market value of something. However, that is not what real property assessment in American cities tends to be in practice. Instead, it is more often a matter of ascribing a politically acceptable number to a taxable asset. These figures are arrived at amid various political pressures. The equity and efficiency of the property tax is considered, not in itself, but in its modern role as an unpopular tax among other taxes. Nevertheless, cities continue to put out figures which they claim to be the "market value" of land and improvements. Thus, although public assessments are what land value tax advocates have to work with, their suitability as a starting point for that reform is almost always problematic.

Many jurisdictions are legally required to publish separate assessments for land and improvements. This is a holdover from the days when the property tax was a more important revenue source (and much more public revenue went to local government rather than to higher levels) — and was pioneered by Georgist assessors W. A. Somers and Lawson Purdy. If assessors were actually interested in timely and accurate market values, they would *need* to consider land and buildings separately, because land and building values are influenced by different factors. In general, land tends to appreciate in value over time, while buildings tend to depreciate. Buildings lose value unless they are maintained, and their value increases only when they are physically improved.* On the other hand, land values are affected by shifts in population and trends in the overall economy. The land value and building value figures reported by major cities are often wildly inconsistent — and, even when the full market value of real estate is reported accurately, the building is most often reported as being worth far more than it would bring on the open market. Often, old residential buildings,

---

* Unless they possess singular historical significance. Essentially, *every* parcel of land possesses singular historical significance: it is unique and irreplaceable.

listed on the assessment rolls as having significant value, are sold and immediately razed to build something bigger. Obviously — since demolition has a cost — such a building's *market* value is actually negative. In such cases the market value of the land is decreased by the cost of destroying the obsolete building.

Political pressures are brought to bear on property taxes to support various urban-policy issues, such as affordable housing, construction in depressed areas, enterprise zones and the like. These political forces sometimes distort property assessments, making them less consistent and pushing them farther away from accurately representing market values. In New York City, for example, the assessed values of one to three-family homes are not allowed to increase by more than 6% in any given year, and cannot increase by more than 20% over any five-year period. This can lead to the odd situation in which a parcel's market value can actually decline in a current year, yet its property tax bill could go up, due to the phasing-in of past increases. Over time, such practices can lead to assessment rolls that are wildly inconsistent, and — assuming one expects them to reflect actual market values — very inaccurate.

The generally chaotic state of real estate assessment in various cities is not to be wondered at. Assessment practices and property tax systems have evolved locally; there has never been any mandate to standardize them. At the turn of the 20th century, however, assessment practices developed and practiced by Single Tax-influenced assessors made significant strides in this beneficial direction. Today's Geographic Information System (GIS) technology would make those techniques even easier.

The property tax is, as we've said, understood to be a tax among other taxes — but, unlike most other taxes, it is administered at the local level. People tend not to like taxation in any form, but the local property tax is the one that groups of voters have the best chance to actually affect. With all the political pressures that are brought to bear on the property tax, it shouldn't be surprising that assessments fall short of the goal of reporting true market values. This leads to a situation in which it is thought that accurate land value assessments *cannot* be done, simply because they *have not* been done. However, the real estate industry has no trouble appraising the value of urban land parcels — knowing, for example, when a building is really a "tear-down." As Ted Gwartney explains in this volume, accurate, consistent urban land assessments are feasible for any competent assessor who has the will (and the institutional support) to do them.

4. Legal obstacles

About half the states in the US have constitutional provisions requiring all forms of property to be taxed at an equal rate. Such "uniformity clauses" are archaic; they stem from attempts by various political blocs to make sure their rivals won't get away with a better tax deal. They are thought to have originated in the Northeast, where small farmers, whose land was their biggest asset, wanted to make sure that urban building owners would not escape taxation. However, slaveholders in the South became an important constituency in favor of tax uniformity. One by one the Southern states moved to replace "poll taxes," which levied a tax on each slave, with property taxes that applied the same rate to all forms of property. This meant that small farmers would bear a larger share of the tax burden. It is ironic that the steps that, for Georgists, begin the process toward economic justice are stymied by a legal roadblock that is largely attributable to the politics of slavery.[*]

Other laws that govern property taxation, restricting reform initiatives, are often enacted at the state level, even though property taxation is administered locally. The upshot of all this is that although the goal of land value tax reform is universal, the first steps toward it must be meticulously tailored to the specific legal situation of each jurisdiction.

5. Poor understanding of the reform's effects

Progress and Poverty is an inspiring book. It offers a vision of social transformation that can begin, not with a violent revolution, but with a simple tax reform initiative. Unfortunately, though, this simple tax reform has proved difficult to sell. When progress does get made, LVT advocates are understandably excited. This can tempt them to make extravagant claims about the reform's effects.

The main problem, at the introductory level, is a misconception about the effect of the reform on land prices, rents and housing costs. Henry George predicted that the "sovereign remedy" would, by eliminating the economic cancer of land speculation, make housing

---

[*]   See Einhorn, *American Taxation, American Slavery*

much more affordable, effectively raising wages at the expense of rents. It would seem reasonable to assume that a modest step in the direction of Henry George's remedy would yield a modest bit of the results he predicted. In other words, if a city were to increase taxes on land and decrease taxes on buildings, land speculation would be a bit more expensive, land would come onto the market at lower prices and housing would become more affordable. Unfortunately, this simple progression ignores important dynamic effects — which are clearly predicted in theory and observed in fact. Evidently the Georgist remedy must be implemented to a sufficient degree before the economy-wide effects Henry George predicted can take place.

An initial step in that direction, such as municipal two-rate property tax reform, cannot be assumed to function like a "mini single tax." Many studies show that the main effect of a tax shift off of buildings and onto land results is increased construction. Cities that adopt this reform enjoy increases in building permits during periods in which comparable cities do not. This is a very good thing; for example, LVT was held to be the biggest factor in the transformation of Harrisburg, Pennsylvania from one of the most distressed cities in the US to a prosperous, growing capital city. However, there is no basis for assuming that LVT will raise wages, beyond a temporary surge in employment brought on by new construction. And, two-rate property tax reform clearly does not lower land values; in fact, it tends to increase them.

The vision of the Single Tax is that land rent belongs to the community. Therefore, Georgists may think the most important aspect of LVT reform is to collect more land rent for public revenue. However, in its initial stages, the more economically important aspect of LVT is lower taxes on buildings. This is because the tax on the rent of land is economically neutral (land rent must be paid anyway; what rent the government does not collect must be paid to the private landowner) whereas the tax on buildings is simply a deadweight loss that increases the annual cost of buildings. People are willing to pay more for land in cities that tax buildings less. The initial effect of LVT reforms in many jurisdictions has been to increase land values. This has been cited as one of the reasons for the failure of national land value taxation in Denmark in 1959-60.† Danish advocates contended

---

† See Tholstrup, *"Economic Liberalism"*

that the reform would decrease land prices; although it had other extremely beneficial economic effects, such as higher wages, lower inflation, trade surpluses, etc., it manifestly did not lower land values.

If the introduction of LVT increases land values, it is conceivable that it would not only not deter land speculation, but actually encourage it. If the "incentive taxation" brought about a wave of revitalization that increased land values more than increased public recovery of rent decreased them, land values would go up. Mason Gaffney notes that local LVT can lead to local governments and improvement districts becoming land speculators, by issuing municipal bonds backed by land values they expect to appreciate.[*] Some vacant or underutilized land would be brought into use, of course — but some more might be held out of use in hope of appreciation. It is noteworthy that Pittsburgh, after decades of its graded tax policy, under which land value was taxed 2.6 times more than building value, still had to embark on an extensively subsidized urban renewal program in the early 1950s to relieve blight in its "Golden Triangle" downtown area.[†]

An even clearer example of this process is seen in New York City's exemption of new housing from taxation, 1921-1931, while continuing to tax land values (and, during this period, New York's land assessments, under the influence of Georgist assessor Lawson Purdy, accurately reflected true market values). The policy was spectacularly successful, vastly increasing New York City's housing stock, and population — and substantially increasing land values. There is some evidence that the effects of the Great Depression were milder in Pittsburgh and New York than in other cities. Land values in Pittsburgh did not fall nearly as far as they did in other cities, according to Percy Williams, and New York's population continued to rise during the 1930s, while other Northeastern cities did not, according to Mason Gaffney. This is usually attributed to Governor Al Smith's tax-abatement policy. However, Gaffney showed in *New Life in Old Cities* that highly accurate land assessments were an equally important factor.

---

[*] Letter to the writer from Prof. Gaffney

[†] See Williams. "The Pittsburgh Graded Tax Plan"

Where do we go from here?

This list of challenges seems daunting. One might be tempted to conclude that the Georgist remedy is a wonderful theoretical possibility, yet unlikely to be realized. One response to this has been a sort of dogged purism, a sense that nothing else will work, that this is the "Sovereign Remedy" and sooner or later society must either adopt it or, as Agnes deMille warned, "enter a new dark age." Henry George himself seemed to share this feeling when he wrote, in *Progress and Poverty*,

> *But for those who see Truth and would follow her; for those who recognize Justice and would stand for her, success is not the only thing. Success! Why, Falsehood has often that to give; and Injustice often has that to give....*

But, of course, it is not enough to smugly know "the answer" and abjure responsibility for making it happen, as society slides deeper into political and ecological chaos, and the problem of poverty amid plenty goes unsolved. Progress needs to be made. Strategies must be planned, tactics identified. What steps need to be taken, by what actors, at what levels, to get us closer to our goal of establishing a just and prosperous economic order?

The first on our list of difficulties, public ignorance and indifference, must be addressed by a coherent, competent and well-resourced popular education effort. This book assumes that such an effort is already well underway: it is intended as a catalogue of implementation strategies, to be read by students who already understand the basics of Georgist political economy.

However, popular education efforts must be a big part of any implementation strategy. The conventional wisdom treats such topics as land, taxation, wealth, economic growth and welfare in ways that make it difficult for Georgist analysis to even cross people's radar screens, much less be taken seriously. This is why our education efforts must have both breadth — as wide a reach as the full spectrum of 21st-century media affords, and depth — enough theoretical grounding to hold our own in debates.

The issues and methods of Georgist education are, for the most part, outside the scope of this volume. Nevertheless, the first steps toward applying land value taxation must be educational. Citizens, politicians, and even many economists simply don't know what LVT advocates are talking about. Advocates need to understand Georgist theory well enough to adapt it to various circumstances and various kinds of entrenched opposition.

A role for citizen economists

Enthusiasm has been growing, in recent years, for the contributions of "citizen scientists." People who are interested in a scientific topic, but lack formal training, nevertheless work on studies, gather data or take part in experiments. This sort of thing has not been seen, however, in economics, which is felt to be an esoteric discipline, understood only by elite practitioners.

The Georgist paradigm, however, doesn't depend on secret knowledge.* It can, of course, have subtle ramifications — but its basic insights are evident enough to be drawn by a civilian's brush. With a grounding in basic Georgist theory, and access to the Internet, any LVT advocate can offer useful support to a campaign for LVT reform.

Many cities (and other jurisdictions) publish real estate assessment data that are essentially fictitious. This presents a problem for LVT advocates. However, one way we know how far off the assessment data are is that we can examine them: they are public information. For the most part, assessment rolls are used by individual real estate owners to examine (and often to protest) their own tax assessments. However, they can be compared with sales data to show the trends by which land is mis-assessed (and under-taxed). Examples can be made public to demonstrate the potential amounts of land rent that are available. Such examples can serve as very effective discussion-starters about the potential of land rent as a revenue source. They can also illustrate our economic justice argument by very clearly showing how much unearned income is gleaned by the passive owners of prime urban sites.

The relationship of public infrastructure spending to land values (and the effects of land speculation in areas made valuable

---

* The author once came up with a laugh line, introducing a paper on urban property assessments at an economic conference: "Many of the papers presented here today make extensive use of mathematics. Mine is a bit different; it makes extensive use of arithmetic."

by such spending) is another area that lends itself to powerful demonstration. A "connect the dots" presentation using examples of this relationship is a very effective way of getting people to notice economic facts that are right in front of their noses. Such presentations can be offered to many kinds of public forums, and, of course, the more such discussions bounce around on the Internet, the more people will start to "see the cat."

The challenges facing Georgist activists are daunting, but not insuperable. We can take heart in the fact that a growing number of prominent economists have written approvingly of the rent-as-revenue idea. Our message needs marketing, but the emergence of new media offers us historic opportunities to do just that. I hope that this book will inspire readers with a clearer understanding of what can be done to move society in the direction of the Georgist remedy.[†]

[†] SEEING THE CAT" has long been a slang term for achieving an understanding of Henry George's ideas. Louis F. Post, in his book *The Prophet of San Francisco*, quotes a speech made by Judge James G. Maguire in the 1880s: "I was one day walking along Kearney Street in San Francisco when I noticed a crowd in front of a show window... I took a glance myself, but I saw only a poor picture of an uninteresting landscape. As I was turning away my eye caught these words underneath the picture: 'Do you see the cat?' ...I spoke to the crowd. "Gentlemen, I do not see a cat in the picture; is there a cat there?" Someone in the crowd replied, "Naw, there ain't no cat there. Here's a crank who says he sees a cat in it, but none of the rest of us can." Then the crank spoke up. "I tell you," he said, "there is a cat there. The picture is all cat. What you fellows take for a landscape is nothing more than a cat's outlines. And you needn't call a man a crank either because he can see more with his eyes than you can with yours."

Assessment of Land Values

by Ted Gwartney

I. The Nature of Land and Natural Resources

Land, in an economic sense, is defined as the entire material universe outside of people and their products. It includes all natural resources, materials, airwaves, as well as the ground. All air, soil, minerals and water, every type of natural opportunity, is categorized as land.

Land's uniqueness stems from its fixed supply, its immobility and its indispensability: it cannot be manufactured or reproduced, and it is required directly or indirectly in the production of all goods and services. All people, at all times, must make use of land. Land has no cost of production. It is nature's gift, which enables life to continue and prosper.

Land rent is the price paid annually for the exclusive right (a monopoly) to use a certain location, piece of land or other natural resource. Equity and efficiency require that the general public, the community that created land value, should be paid for the exclusive use of a land site. The basic form of that payment is a land value tax.

Many people labor under the misapprehension that land rent contributes only a small portion of total value. But, as societies progress, land's economic influence increases, until it becomes the predominant force in determining the progress or poverty within a community. Land in major cities is so costly that people are forced to move farther away and travel great distances in order to get to work and social attractions. In the more developed countries of the world, land rent represents at least 25% of gross annual production, and most likely more than 40%.[*]

Labor and capital are variable in supply. A higher price for commodities — and buildings — causes more labor and capital to make itself available. Labor is rewarded for its work, and capital for its contribution to production. A high price is an incentive to work harder and longer. However, because land is fixed in supply, its rent serves no such incentive function. Therefore, economic rent is the only source of public revenue that has no negative effect on the productive potential of the economy. Economically, rent is a surplus. When a community captures land rent for public purposes, both efficiency and equity are realized. This implies that public revenue should not be supplied by taxes, such as income or wage taxes; sales, commodity or value-added taxes, until all of the available revenue has been first collected from the natural and community created value of land.[†]

Not only is land rent a potentially important source of public revenue, the tax on land is a means of limiting speculation in land prices. This would keep land from being held out of use, ensuring that all citizens have an equal opportunity to be productive. People could invest in productive equipment and wages, rather than in high land prices which produce no additional tangible wealth.

---

[*] In most nations the data needed to calculate this figure is largely absent. Terry Dwyer's 2003 study of Australia, which does collect land assessment data at the national level, arrived at the 40% figure. Studies by Mason Gaffney, particularly his "The Taxable Capacity of Land: Enough and to Spare" suggest that the aggregate figure for the United States is at least 40%. Prof. Nicolaus Tideman adds that "In my opinion, such a calculation is not what we should be interested in, because if all of the rent of land were collected publicly, land would have no selling price, and there would be no annual increase in its value." Also, Henry George explains in Book IX of *Progress and Poverty* that the economic vitality that would likely be created by a shift to public collection of land rent in lieu of other taxes would eventually increase aggregate rent by a significant amount.

[†] In considering how the rent fund should be apportioned, Georgist economists note the distinction between values created purely by nature, such as that of a unique location for a sheltered harbor, and those created by human effort, such as public infrastructure. See Tideman, "Integrating Land Value Taxation..."

Land Value Belongs to the Community

Land has market value for three reasons: 1) the limited supply and "natural" productivity of the soil and natural resources; 2) the publicly provided services, including planning, improvements that increase the market value of land; 3) the growth of communities and peoples' competitive demand for the exclusive use of prime locations.

Land rent is the price that people and businesses are willing to pay for the exclusive right to possess and use a good land site for a period of time. It is a measure of the benefit an individual receives from the exclusive use of a land site. For example, people prefer to use sites of good location because it gives them an advantage of spending less time in travel by being near what they choose to do and where they work. A business can sell more goods at a site where many people pass each day, compared to a site where only a few people would pass.

The full community, along with nature, creates land's value — and secures its exclusive use. The collection of land rent for public revenue returns this value to the community.

When a major part of land rent is not collected, which is the case in most of the world today, the value of the public improvements becomes an asset which landholders enjoy, although they did nothing to create it. The community added to the market value of land by making improvements which increases demand for the land. The longer the possessors hold the land out of use, the greater will be the bonus they obtain.

By prohibiting people from using good land, the possessors force the premature use of other less desirable land, more distant from the city center. This raises the cost of community improvements and the rental value of the unused, but better located, land. This precipitates the degradation of the rural environment by using city land inefficiently — and creates huge unnecessary pressures on the natural environment. This process of urban sprawl also creates unnecessarily high infrastructure and transportation costs. That is because failure to collect land rent subsidizes the waste of natural resources and clutters the environment. Cities that collect the full rental value of land are more compact and provide better, less costly amenities for their citizens.

When the rent of the land is not collected for public revenue, any moves to enact good government principles must be, to some extent, self-defeating. As a city becomes more pleasant and prosperous, and its population grows, its land becomes more valuable. When people can make a larger profit by doing nothing, but keeping the land they possess out of use for a long period of time, they will do so. When the community collects the full market rent of land, they eliminate the motive for keeping land out of efficient use.

The major function of a competent city government is to provide good community services by collecting the land rent created within the community to ensure the efficient use of land and equal opportunities for all of its citizens. Transportation is an important function of government which would facilitate the creation of a compact city, where people can easily find the facilities they desire for education, commerce, religion and recreation. Good land use, with the freedom of individuals to achieve the highest and best use of land, would ensure a desirable community. A compact city would reduce the need to invade the wilderness and devastate the environment.

Efficiency of Public Revenue

Adam Smith, in *Wealth of Nations*, suggested that any "tax" should be a charge for services which are more efficiently performed by the community than by individual efforts. He postulated four principles of taxation which any source of revenue should meet. As much as possible, a source of public revenue should be:

1. Light on the production of wealth, and does not impede or reduce production;
2. Cheap to collect, requiring few collectors, and easy to understand;
3. Certain; can't be avoided, little opportunity for corruption, and provides adequate revenue;
4. Equitable and fair, payment for benefits received, impartial, just.

Land rent is the only public-revenue source that meets all of these criteria. It has been argued that the difficulty of accurate and fair land value assessment renders land value taxation unsuitable under criteria 2, 3 and possibly 4, above. However, this is due to misconceptions about land assessment that will be addressed in the remainder of this paper. As an assessor, I found that valuing the land was the least difficult part of making a property assessment. In addition to vacant land sales, every improved property sale included a sale of land. By removing the building value portion, the land sale price was apparent. Land values are consistent within a neighborhood except for obvious differences for which adjustments can be made.

How Much Rent Should the Community Collect?

In order to preserve the environment, it is necessary to make more efficient use of our existing communities. Efficient land use fails under most contemporary land systems. Few communities have collected enough of their land rent to effectively curb land speculation and create a just and prosperous economy.

Studies have demonstrated that communities prosper and succeed in proportion to the percentage of the land rent that they collect. The first communities that decide to collect all of the ground rent will have an enormous competitive advantage over other similar communities. They will be able to reduce or eliminate regressive taxes on labor and capital. They will attract new business and industry and become prosperous.

How much land rent should the community collect? Let's consider the alternatives. Whatever is not collected will be capitalized into land value — and the cost of land at inflated market prices is a block to new industry. To maintain an equitable society, where nobody has special benefits that they do not pay for, it is important for the community to collect all of the land rent. It should use what is needed for public services and improvements such as schools, hospitals, parks, police, roadways, utilities and defense — and reserve a fund for emergencies. If there is excess revenue, not needed for public facilities and services, it could be distributed to each citizen in that community equally.

Land Rent Compared with Market Value

The market value of land is the land's rental value, minus land taxes, divided by a capitalization rate. Each of these terms is defined as follows:

Land Rental Value is the annual fee individuals are willing to pay for the exclusive right to use a land site for a period of time. This may include a speculative opportunity cost.

Land Taxes (or Land Rent Revenue) is the portion of the land rental value that is claimed for the community.

Capitalization Rate is a market determined rate of return that would attract individuals to invest in the use of land, considering all of the risks and benefits which could be realized.

Land Market Value is the land rental value, minus land taxes, divided by a capitalization rate.

The mathematical relationship is then:

$$\text{Land Market Value} = \frac{\text{Land Rental Value - Land Taxes}}{\text{Capitalization Rate}}$$

Land Rental Value = Market Value x Capitalization Rate + Land Taxes

For example, assume that the land rent for a site is $1,800, the land taxes are $300 and the capitalization rate is 6%, what would the land market value be?

$$\text{Land Market Value} = \frac{\$1,800 - \$300}{6\%} = \frac{\$1,500}{6\%} = \$25,000$$

What would result if a larger portion of the land rent were collected? Let's consider $1,650 rather than $300.

$$\text{Land Market Value} = \frac{\$1,800 - \$1,650}{6\%} = \frac{\$150}{6\%} = \$2,500$$

If any three factors are known, the fourth can be calculated. Land rental value can be used instead of market value, or vice versa, in the discussion of land assessment systems.

If a smaller amount of land rent remained to be capitalized after land taxes were collected, land could have a lower market value, but it would continue to have the same rental value.

Principles of Land Assessment

An appraisal is essentially an expert opinion of the market value of a site; the assessor's estimate must be supportable and comprehensible. The assessor must develop and use specific terminology suitable and pertinent to land appraisal.

A land site includes everything within the earth, under its boundaries and over it, extending infinitely into space. In addition to a location for a house or building, a land site would include the minerals, water, trees, view, sunshine and air space. The shape of the site can be described as an inverted cone with its apex at the center of the earth and extending upward through the surface into space.

Conceptually, a land site extends infinitely into space, but its value cannot be infinite. The assessment process is essentially the valuation of rights to use or possess specific aspects of land sites. Such rights include subsurface mineral rights, riparian (water) rights, grazing rights, timber rights, fishing rights, hunting rights, access rights and air rights.

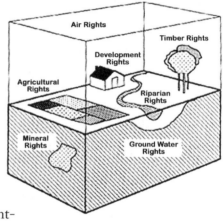

In appraisal, a land site is a parcel of land that is finished and ready for use under the standards prevailing in its area. It might have the necessary public utilities in place, like gas, electricity, water, telephone and sewer, with streets, sidewalks drainage and grading completed.

The assessor bases his estimate of market value upon basic economic principles. There are many economic principles which people and assessors must understand and use when implementing judgment to estimate land market values. It is necessary to discuss a few of the more important principles.

The principle of **substitution** maintains that the value of a land parcel tends to be set by the price that a person would have to pay to acquire an equally desirable substitute property, assuming that no expensive delay is encountered in making the substitution. A person would pay no more for a site than would have to be paid for an equally desirable site.

The principle of **supply and demand** holds that the value of a site will increase if the demand increases. Because the supply, in this case, remains fixed, land's value varies directly with demand.

The principle of **anticipation** contends that land value can go up or down in anticipation of a future benefit or detriment.

The principle of **conformity** contends that land will achieve its maximum value when it is used in a way that conforms to the existing economic and social standards within a neighborhood.

Utility, Scarcity and Desirability

Land value can be thought of as the relationship between a desired location and a potential user. The ingredients that constitute land value are utility, scarcity and desirability. These factors must all be present for land to have value.

Land that lacks utility and scarcity also lacks value, since utility arouses desire for use and has the power to give satisfaction. The air we breathe has utility; however, in the economic sense, air is not valuable because it hasn't been appropriated and there is enough for everyone. Thus there is no scarcity — at least at the moment. This may not be true in the future, however, as knowledge of air pollution and its effect on human health make people aware that clean and breathable air may become scarce and subsequently valuable.

By themselves, utility and scarcity confer no value on land. There must also be demand: the potential user must be able to participate in the market to satisfy their desire.

Limitations on Land Ownership and Use

While land is the gift of nature, most societies impose legal, political and social constraints on its ownership and use. Four forms of governmental control include:

Taxation — Power to tax the land to provide public revenue and to return to the community the costs incurred to pay for the various public benefits, services and environmental protection, which are provided by the government;

Eminent Domain — Right to use, hold or take land for common public uses and benefits;

Police Power — Right to regulate land use for the welfare of the public, in the areas of safety, health, morals, general welfare, zoning, building codes, traffic regulations and sanitary regulations;

Escheat — Right to have land revert to the public's agent, the government, when taxes are not paid or when there are no legal heirs.

Factors that Contribute to Land Value

Physical attributes of land include quality of location, fertility and climate; convenience to shopping, schools and parks; availability of water, sewers, utilities and public transportation; absence of bad smells, smoke and noise; and patterns of land use, frontage, depth, topography, streets and lot sizes.

Legal or governmental forces include the type and amount of taxation, zoning and building laws, planning and restrictions.

Social factors include population growth or decline, changes in family sizes, typical ages, attitudes toward law and order, prestige and education levels.

Economic forces include value and income levels, growth and new construction, vacancy and availability of land. It is the influences of these forces, expressed independently and in relationship to one another, that help the people and the assessor measure value.

Highest and Best Use of Land

A land site should be made available to the users who can make the highest and best effective use of the site — which serves to maximize the site benefits for all people. The proper system of assessment and taxation of land can provide for the proper economic use of the land. A high land tax on an improperly improved site tends to cause the site holder to either better improve his site or to look for someone else with the means to properly improve the site. Before an assessment can proceed, the highest and best use must be determined for each site.

Estimating the highest, best and most profitable use of land is the goal of the assessment process. Highest and best use is restricted to uses that are legally permissible (meeting zoning, health, and public restrictions), physically possible (has adequate size, soil conditions, and accessibility), and economically feasible (income is anticipated). The use that meets these criteria and produces the greatest net earnings (best returns) is the highest and best use.

Procedures for Land Assessment

An assessment (or an appraisal) is essentially an opinion of value made by an experienced knowledgeable person. Assessors base their estimate of land market value upon basic economic principles which serve as the foundation of the valuation process. Anyone can learn how to do this — and learn to do it more accurately.

The assessment or appraisal process is an organized procedural analysis of data. This procedure involves six specific phases, each of which contains numerous procedures.

1. Defining the Assignment

The goal is to estimate the market value of all land sites within a given district. This will include manufacturing enterprises, apartments, commercial enterprises, single family home sites, government land, farms and all other land and natural resources of various descriptions.

The assessor should be able to support his estimate of land market, both in discussion and in writing. The assessor must define and use specific terminology suitable and pertinent to land appraisal. Economic Land Rent was defined as the value paid or imputed for the exclusive right to use a land site location or natural resources for a period of time, generally one year.

2. Determining the Data Required and Its Source

A land market assessment system is based upon data related to land attributes. These data generally include maps, aerial photographs, descriptions of physical characteristics such as size, shape, view and topography; permitted uses, present uses, available utilities, proximity to town centers or employment and site improvements like streets, curbs, gutters, sidewalks and street lights. Governments have much of this data available; in many cases these data can easily be plotted on GIS maps.

How are values or acquisition fees currently being determined and paid by land occupiers? Are records being maintained for these values or fees? If land market values have been estimated in the past, attempts should be made to build upon the existing systems, while making constant improvements to data collection.

3. Collecting and Recording the Data

Many governments do not have all of this information available in a single data base. Assessors must determine:

1) what land data and valuation systems currently exist
2) how effectively they operate
3) how to build upon and improve these systems
4) how to implement procedures for collecting additional data

Effective land revenue systems can be created, even if no valuation system is currently in place. Assessors can begin by ascertaining what land data presently exists and how it could be assembled for use in a land valuation system. They should collect and maintain the data needed from any existing records, even though they are not currently stored in a single source. They should determine what additional data would be valuable and where it can be obtained. They should develop procedures for collecting any additional data required to determine land market values and the data should be collected for the differences in characteristics for each site.

The assessor may train a small team to find and record the additional desired data. The data should be displayed in a useful manner such as on a GIS map. In an area with no systems or data in place, simple relationships could be drawn for permitted use (zone), distance to amenities (location), physical characteristics (size, topography, view, and so on) and other significant factors. Data could be collected and analyzed on a neighborhood and type of potential use basis.

Conversations with residents and businessmen could help to define the parameters which people in the local community use to determine favorable land location. An interview might reveal that the distance to transportation, such as a river, roadway or public transportation, weighs greatly in people's minds. Or, other factors may predominate, such as homogeneity of a neighborhood or distance to shopping and schools. Planners, government officials, real estate agents, appraisers and others involved in real estate may also provide useful data.

Even if no land sales or market evidence exists, the specific factors which influence land market value are well understood by most people in any area, even in primitive cultures. The assessor's job is one of skillfully determining the relative priorities identified by local people.

A sample of typical and varied land sites within a city could be selected to demonstrate a land valuation system. Based upon a study, land market values could be assigned by a competent assessor. The assessor could use a few people trained to collect and analyze existing data, then analyze the sample survey data and set standards for the base market values in the area. The difference in market value of the attributes that enhance or detract from a typical site could be added or subtracted to the base market value for the other sites in the study. These features should be recorded on the land market map, which would show the primary sites with markets declining as desirability decreases or increasing as desirability increases.

Several examples of land assessment systems will be discussed in this paper, from a simple example with no significant land data, to a more complex example with plentiful land data. The methods employed will depend upon the land market data that currently exists and how that data can be assembled for use in a land assessment system.

4. Verifying the Data

Since the assessor's opinion of market value is not based upon personal experience, the data should be verified with two different sources. Market data should be verified with a person directly involved in the transaction. For example, one party could be the agent representing the seller. Another party could be the site user who agrees to the sale amount. Additional sources might be government land agents or officials who have firsthand knowledge of the sale. If the data is made available to the public, inaccuracies can also be brought to light by concerned citizens.

Analyzing and Interpreting the Data

The balance of this report will be concentrated on various methods of analyzing and interpreting land market data. Several methods will be suggested to secure the goal of estimating the market value of all land sites.

1. Estimating the Market Values

Once the analysis has been concluded, it will be possible for the assessor to make a rational estimate of the market value of every land site. This estimate will serve as the basis for the value that will be paid by a site user for the exclusive use of a site. The assessor would assign preliminary land value estimates based upon the comparative estimated usefulness and desirability of the sites. Initially, they could accomplish this task in a general manner, with the understanding that refinements would be made to reflect new information and public opinion.

2. Public Examination and Analysis of the Land Market Values

The preliminary land value assessment for each site could then be displayed on a land value map. Public examination and analysis of the market values for land sites would help to clarify any errors in assessments. People who occupy land acquire skills in noticing slight differences in land characteristics. They can explain to the assessor why and how differences should be reflected in the conclusions about land values.

Once an adequate sample survey has been completed and had favorable public review, the result can be used throughout the total area. These sample data results could be used to estimate the comparative markets of each land site.

To ensure the optimal and equitable use of land sites, land assessments should reflect the highest and best use of each site.

3. Periodic Updating of Assessments

Land market values tend to increase each year, usually at a rate greater than inflation. Building values tend to decline each year, because of a wearing out of the physical structure and/or its functional desirability. If assessments are not maintained on a regular basis (annually) land will become greatly under-assessed and buildings will be over-assessed in only a few years. Additionally, the federal tax deductibility of building depreciation leads to a tendency to overassess buildings relative to land. Over time these processes can lead to large distortions that impair both equity and efficiency.

Three Approaches to Valuing Real Estate

The first step in the valuation of land is determining the highest and best use of the site. Again, the four criteria that highest and best use must meet are: physically possible, legally permissible, financially feasible, and maximally productive. Two types of analyses are made in determining the highest and best use. The first is the highest and best use of the site, if vacant; the second is the highest and best use of the site as improved, or if undeveloped as proposed to be improved.

There are three standard approaches to estimating market value that form the foundation for current appraisal theory: the cost approach, the sales comparison approach and the income approach.

The **cost approach** is based upon the principle that the informed purchaser would pay no more than the cost to acquire a substitute property with the same utility as the subject property. It is particularly applicable when the property being appraised involves relatively new improvements which represent the highest and best use of the land, or when relatively unique or specialized improvements are located on the site and for which there exists no comparable properties on the market.

The **sales comparison approach** utilizes prices paid in actual market transactions of similar properties to estimate the value of the site. This appraisal technique is dependent upon utilizing truly comparable market or sales data which have occurred near enough in time to reflect market conditions relative to the time period of the appraisal. This method could also be used to estimate the rental value.

The **income capitalization approach** is widely applied in appraising income-producing properties. Anticipated present and future net operating income, as well as any future reversions, are discounted to a present worth figure through the capitalization process. This approach also relies upon market data to establish current rental rates and expense levels to arrive at an expected net operating income. If, however, a site is not being put to its highest and best use, the capitalization of its current income cannot yield an accurate estimation of its true market value.

The resulting indications of value from the three approaches to value are correlated into a final estimate of value for the site. It is not always practicable to use all three approaches to value. The nature of the property being appraised, and the amount, quality, and type of data available dictate the use of one or more of the three approaches. Variations of the three approaches to value can be devised. Several will be presented in this paper.

Specific Methods Used in Appraising Land Value

The most reliable way to estimate land value is by sales comparison. When few sales are available or when the value indications produced through sales comparison require substantiation, other procedures may be used to value land. In all, seven procedures can be used to obtain land value indications.

Sales comparison — Sales of similar, vacant parcels are analyzed, compared, and adjusted to provide a value indication for the land being appraised.

Proportional Relationship — Relating a site to a known standard site. The difference can be expressed as a percentage. This procedure can be used when their is little value evidence in existence.

Land Residual Technique: Hypothetical Building — Land value is estimated by developing a hypothetical building of the highest and best use for a given site. Estimate the gross possible income, deduct all operating expenses and the income attributable to buildings and other agents of production. The net income imputed to the land is capitalized to derive an estimate of land value.

Allocation — Sales of improved properties are analyzed, and the prices paid are allocated between the land and the improvements.

Land Residual Technique: Actual Building Extraction — Land value is estimated by subtracting the estimated value of the depreciated improvements from the known sale price of the property. Improvement Value can be estimated by income capitalization.

Ground Rent Capitalization — This procedure is used when land rental and capitalization rates are readily available, as in well-developed areas. Net ground rent — the net amount paid for the right to use and occupy the land — is estimated and divided by a land capitalization rate.

Subdivision Development — The total value of undeveloped land is estimated as if the land were subdivided, developed, and sold. Development costs, incentive costs, and carrying charges are subtracted from the estimated proceeds of sale, and the net income projection is discounted over the estimated period required for market absorption of the developed sites.

With the appraisal process and the approaches to value understood, it is appropriate to consider the methods and procedures used to analyze and interpret the land data. The choice is based upon what data is available, its reliability and usefulness in making a value estimate.

The land market is not a perfect market, but is made up of the expressions of all different types of persons in terms of money in relation to potential land use. The assessor uses market sales and site data to estimate what value would be paid for a site, assuming a competitive market involving knowledgeable people who are typically motivated and acting in their own best interest.

Standard Units of Measure

Land markets can be estimated on the basis of a certain value per unit and the unit is often one of the following:

Per Dwelling Unit site
Per square-foot
Per acre
Per front-foot

The selection of the most appropriate unit, or combination of units, is important. Land is not always sold on the same basis, but rather on the value in the eyes of the user. Therefore, the assessor must be careful to choose the appropriate unit of measure. This can help in the interpretation of market evidence for a few sites (the sample), so that all of the sites can be properly estimated (the population).

For example, the user of a condominium unit will share the use of a large site, but a certain air space will belong to them and command a different market value due to height, access, view and preference. In urban land valuation, many of the sites to be valued will be of similar sizes and arranged in more-or-less orderly rows on streets, avenues, boulevards and cul-de-sacs. Many will be of identical size with minor departures arising from topography and shape. The assessor will probably wish to adopt a standard site value, which includes the majority of sites, for the particular area under review — standard both as to probable market value and to characteristics.

The standard residential site may respond well to a value Per Dwelling Unit Site. A commercial use may be better estimated by using a value Per Square-Foot or Per Front-Foot. A farm or rural site may be better estimated by using a value Per Acre. Once the market value per unit of measure has been established for the standard site representative of the area, the value will become a base to which all other sites can be compared.

Adjustments will have to be made for differences between the standard site and every other site. The assessor will want to study the typical differences and make individual refinements. There may be reasons for an increase in value for characteristics which are better than the standard site. They would make a positive adjustment for desirable characteristics, such as superior location, view, topography, services or access.

There can also be reasons for loss of value for characteristics which are inferior to the standard site. They would make a negative adjustment for undesirable characteristics, such as poor location, longer distance to transportation, longer distance to the civic center, wet ground in the winter, overabundance of rock or poor access

Site valuation may be summed up in the manner of a Unity Rating which will be X% greater or less than unity (1.0) when compared with the base standard site characteristics adopted for tile area.

Standardized Adjustments

Typically, a comparative method is applied to land markets under review. Adjustments are made for divergences from the standard site by the use of a specific set of rules. The most common examples are those used for distance and size. The methods were born out of the necessity to produce sound and impartial market estimates in a limited amount of time.

It is essential to use discretion and judgment and only treat standardized methods as guides. The use of formulas should be the result of local market analysis and testing. Sales are sought that are similar except for the one difference that is being analyzed. The main virtue of this method is its administrative adaptability, permitting land markets to be estimated on the basis of strict comparability. Mistakes become more easily detectable, particularly in cases of errors of judgment and mathematics.

Following is an example of an adjustment grid and tile procedures which are commonly used to estimate site value after considering all differences. This shows how market values increase or decrease due to distance, size, frontage and other important characteristic differences.

Sales evidence will frequently indicate that minor variations in sites, whether frontage or size, have little effect on markets. The assessor could select the standard Dwelling Unit site, both as to location and market. They would proceed to make judgment decisions in relating the other sites to the site that was selected as the standard site — rating them as standard, superior or inferior. The **Per Dwelling Unit Site** method is useful in the valuation of apartments and homes. It may also be combined with the use of another method such as the per square-foot method.

Adjustments for Unique Features

After the base value has been estimated, the individual sites must be considered. Some sites have unique advantages or disadvantages compared to other sites. Actual real estate market values vary for each site and are dependent upon numerous individual features, qualities, characteristics and restrictions such as:

location	zoning	site	access
utilities	use density	view	frontage
topography	river	transportation	parks
traffic	regulations	noise	utilities

People would tend to be willing to pay additional value for a land site with special advantages and would pay less value for a land site with disadvantages. The market value for the unique differences would be determined by how much more or less site users in general were willing to pay for those features. This market difference must be determined for each significant variable feature.

Per dwelling unit site

VARIABLE	=	STANDARD	>	SUPERIOR	<	INFERIOR
Base Value - $		$80,000		$80,000		$80,000
Downtown - miles	5	0	3	+ 4,000	7	- 4,000
Size - square feet	10,000	0	12,000	+ 4,000	8,000	- 4,000
Transport - blocks	3	0	1	+ 8,000	6	- 6,000
Recreation - blocks	6	0	3	+ 4,000	10	- 3,000
Adjusted value - $		$80,000		$100,000		$63,000

The difference can then be converted to an adjustment of value. For example, if a site were better than the standard in a district because of distance to downtown of 5% ($4,000), site size of 5% ($4,000), location of transportation 10% ($8,000) and convenience of recreation of 5% ($4,000), the site being appraised would be 25% ($20,000) superior to the standard site. In reality most sites have many small differences, both positive and negative, from a standard site.[*]

Sales Adjustment Grid

Per Square-Foot — The value per square-foot unit of measure has application in estimating value for commercial and industrial lands where the applied rate will be more constant over the entire site. The size of the site limits or enhances the use and market value of a site. The application of a market value per square-foot to residential lands is not common, except in dense urban centers.

Per Front-Foot — This method has been useful in the downtown portion of intensely developed cities where people pay a premium for exposure to customers. For those sites that are not identical to the standard site, it will be necessary to make appropriate adjustments for variations in width, depth and other attributes that differ from the standard site. The total departures from standard front-foot market can be expressed as an adjusted frontage. It is against this adjusted frontage that the adopted front-foot value will be applied.

There is a principle of commerce that commodities are cheaper by the dozen. By the same token it could be that frontage feet are cheaper per unit when the total exceeds the average, or standard width. A width table is a series of percentage adjustments greater or less than 1.0 needed to adjust the actual Market per Front-Foot of any site and equate it to the Front-Foot value of the adopted Standard Site.

Per Acre — Beyond the limits of the urban area, where larger parcels are the norm, the unit of measure can best be expressed as a value per acre. The adjustment factors would be completely different however. They might relate to agricultural benefits, such as soil fertility, distance to markets or water supply.

---

[*] Additional land characteristics and assessment information can be found in the manuals published by the International Association of Assessing Officers 314 West 10th Street, Kansas City, Missouri 64105

Proportional Relationship

One method to secure a land assessment system, when sales or rental data is unavailable, is to make an estimate of value based upon the experience in other locations where land data already exists. This is a variation of the Sales Comparison method. It could be used to measure the market value or the rental value of land.

If a jurisdiction has very limited land data, such as permitted use (zoning) and density of population, but no assessment system, it might be possible to build a simple model. An assessor might draw a grid, showing the potential use on the Y axis and the resulting land market value on the X axis.

In this instance, a typical home unit site in a major city could be assigned a base market value of 1.00 to which all other sites would be compared. Moving toward a superior location and potential use would influence the land market value in a positive manner, and vice-versa.

Adjustments for additional attributes and deficiencies could be made for each individual site, after the base market value had been estimated by the comparative method. The experience from a comparative city could be borrowed and tested in the local area to verify the results.

A chart can be created, illustrating the relationship of one type of land use and location, to another site of differing potential land use. The relationships in the chart that follows have been found to be common in many areas of the world. However, every area is different, and a suitable model should be designed by local experts.

This model could be a basis for considering the distinctions that are part of the local society of a city. It should be modified to conform with the local experience. This can be accomplished by performing a local investigation which draws upon the expertise of individuals who understand the advantage that one location has compared to another. A base factor which was equal to the comparative difference could be determined for each use and location. Individual sites could then be adjusted for superior or inferior conditions as compared to the base. A determined value could then apply to all sites, resulting in equitable treatment for varying qualities.

USE - LOCATION	MAJOR CITY	SUBURBAN	DEVELOPING	RURAL
COMMERCIAL				
Central business	20.00+			
Downtown area	10.00	5.00	2.50	
Standard	3.00	2.00	1.00	.75
Secondary	1.50-	1.00	.60	.50
INDUSTRIAL				
Prime	2.50+	1.75	1.50	.95
Standard	1.50	1.00	.75	.65
Inferior	.75-	.50	.40	.25
HOME				
Prime	1.50+	1.00	.75	.50
Standard	1.00	.75	.60	.40
Inferior	.65-	.45	.40	.25
RURAL AND FARMING				
Acreage close-in	.20+	.15	.10	.05
Acreage distant		.10	.05	.02
Intense farming			.03	.02
General farming			.02	.01-

Basis for comparison: An home site of standard quality in a major city = 1.00

Land Residual Technique:
Hypothetical Building

When market or sales data is unavailable, an estimate of the market value of land can be based upon the net land residual income (total income, less all costs except land value). This would result from the development of a hypothetical building of the highest and best use for a given site.

The developmental analysis technique would be used, when the following data can all be reasonably estimated: the best use of the land site, the hypothetical building value, the hypothetical net income to the development and the appropriate capitalization rate.

First, an assessor would determine what hypothetical improvements would represent the highest and best use (greatest net land value) for the site.

Second, to determine the net land income, the assessor would have to estimate the gross possible income which could be earned from the use of the improvements and site combined. An allowance for the average vacancy (non-use) over the life of the investment would be subtracted. Then the probable operating expenses (but excluding income attributable to the land) would be evaluated and deducted.

Third, the assessor would have to estimate the cost of the proposed building. A portion of the net income would be required to recapture the investment in the hypothetical building and furnishings. The remaining income would be income residual to the land.

The selling price would be determined by capitalizing the net income (income which was not collected as land taxes). This would be capitalized at a rate of, say, 6% to estimate the market value of the land. This rate would vary for different types and ages of property. The land price is what a potential future user would have to pay a land owner in order to use the site, unless all of the net rent is used for general community purposes.

An example on a per square foot basis

	Land Income	Land Value
Gross possible income	$24	
Vacancy allowance	-1	
Operating expenses	-5	
Net income before land taxes	$18	$300
Recapture of building cost	-12	200
Land Residual	$6	100
Land Tax	-5	83
Net Land Income	$1	$17

In this example, $6 per square foot is the net land market rent allotted to the land. The land tax is $5 per square foot and the capitalized land value is $17 per square foot.

Allocation

When it is difficult to find vacant land sites that have sold or are offered for sale, the assessor can use an allocation approach. There tends to be a typical ratio of land value to property (land + buildings) value for specific categories of real estate, with similar characteristics, in specific locations.

The individual values for the total property (both the land and building) may be known and available on public records, but there is no allocation made between the land and buildings. Time might best be spent in analyzing a sample of homes to estimate the typical proportion of value which represents land as compared to buildings. This percentage factor could then be applied to all of the total market values for the similar type of homes in a given district, to estimate the individual site land values.

If the existing practice for assigning total values has been arbitrary or not based upon valid market conditions, this method will not be usable. Fairness and justice would require that all markets be based upon a competitive system where all individuals were given an equal opportunity to use a given site. As an interim step, an estimate of competitive total value could be made for different types of property and locations, then an allocation could follow.

The analysis of many units, which represent a random sample, would be conducted, perhaps by using some of the other techniques discussed here. From this analysis a typical land factor (relationship), for each type of property and location, would be determined. The land portion would be allocated from the total value. In the sample below, an assessor might conclude that the typical land factor was .40 (40% land and 60% buildings).

Sample Analysis

Once the portion was determined and tested for accuracy, it could be applied to the entire population of market data for a particular category of real estate in a specific location. At right is an example of such a population application.

Unit number	Total value	- Building portion	= Land portion	Land factor Land/Total %
212	$190,000	$114,000	$76,000	40%
321	$181,000	$105,000	$76,000	42%
222	$192,000	$117,000	$75,000	39%
311	$192,000	$119,000	$73,000	38%
Conclusion: Indicated Land Portion:				40%

Unit number	Total value x	Land factor =	Land value
215	$193,000	.40	$77,200
305	$185,000	.40	$74,000
301	$189,000	.40	$75,600

Land Residual Technique: Actual Building Extraction

The extraction method is a variant of the allocation and developmental methods where the market rent contribution of a building is estimated, then subtracted from the total rent with the balance being assigned as land rent. This was reviewed earlier, and accomplishes a land value analysis in a simplified manner. This could best be used where the improvements or buildings made a small contribution to the rent, and the majority of the value was land value.

	Land Income	Land Value (capitalized)
Gross possible income	$24	
Vacancy allowance	-1	
Operating expenses	-5	
Net income before land taxes	$18	$300
Recapture of building cost	-1	17
Land Residual	$17	-$283
Land Tax	-12	200
Net Land Income	$5	$83

In this example, $5 per square foot is the net land market allotted to the land. The land tax is $12 per square foot and the capitalized land value is $83 per square foot.

Ground Rent Capitalization

In many parts of the world, including areas within the United States, land is owned by an individual or government agency and leased to tenants who construct buildings and pay an annual rental fee. These rental fees can be analyzed just like sales and a market rental fee estimated. This lease fee can be capitalized by an appropriate rate to estimate market value.

Comparable ground rents	Per SF	Location	Traffic	Parking	Adj. SF
Comparable ground rent 1	$10.00	-$0.50	-$0.50	+$0.75	+$9.75
Comparable ground rent 2	$9.50	-$0.25	+$0.50	-$0.25	+$9.50
Comparable ground rent 3	$10.00	-$0.00	-$0.50	+$0.00	+$9.50
Subject market ground rent	$9.50 rent per square foot / 10% = $95.00 value per square foot				

This procedure is used when land rental and capitalization rates are readily available, as in well-developed areas. Net ground rent — the net amount paid for the right to use and occupy the land — is estimated and divided by a land capitalization rate.

Rent 3 was the best comparable located in the same area and required only one adjustment for traffic, Rent 2 required three small adjustments and Rent 1 required larger adjustments. I conclude that the subject land has a value of $9.50 rent per square foot 10% = $95.00 value per square foot.

Subdivision Development

The total value of undeveloped land is estimated as if the land were subdivided, developedand sold.

Total sales proceeds,	
50 sites at $50,000	$2,500,000
Discounted at 15% over 50 months	$1,850,000
Subdivision cost, $1,000 per site	$50,000
Development cost, $15,000 per site	$750,000
Sale cost, 10% of gross sale price	$250,000
Taxes, interest,	
carrying cost, 10% of net value	$50,000
Incentive cost and profit,	
10% of gross sale price	$250,000
Net value of undeveloped land	$500,000
Net value per acre, 12.5 acres	$40,000
Net value per site, 50 sites	$10,000

Development costs, incentive costs and carrying charges are subtracted from the estimated proceeds of sale, and the net income projection is discounted over the estimated period required for market absorption of the developed sites. This is the method used by developers to estimate the price they can pay for raw land.

Technological Improvements

The market values which have been calculated should be displayed on a land market map. Modern Geographic Information Systems (GIS) software can display these value along with the various relevant factors that have been used to arrive at them. This will allow the assessor to review his market data and market value conclusions. One can then judge whether equity has been achieved. A field review will allow him to make further necessary adjustments — for other variables observed in the review — and finish his project. The assessor will find that when the results of his analysis are presented, and the major adjustment criteria utilized, the public can understand the logic of the assessments.

There are many jurisdictions that have both prior market value estimates and some site data available on a computer. They may be capable of using this data as a basis for updating market estimates.

Most government agencies have already collected data about land on a computer system, and sometimes (especially in large cities) this information is made available to the public. By analyzing market trends, new land market estimates could be made with a single updating factor for each permitted land use within a neighborhood.

An entire country would be capable of annual reassessments, updated by computer data entries. A simple model used for computer calculation of land value or market values for 1,000,000 land sites could be based upon a careful analysis of the market value of a sample of 12,000 sites.* A local valuation committee of land experts could define the land use classes, neighborhood areas and market values for each standard site in the area.

The advantages of using moden information technology in land assessment include:

— Facilitating frequent update of markets ensuring equitable treatment of all renters.
— Eliminating arithmetic errors in land value calculations.
— Improving the assessor's productivity in land value assessment.
— Employing standardized assessment techniques that have proven to be effective.

Good Assessments Can — and Must — Be Done

It is to be hoped that, in outlining the basic principles and techniques of land assessment, this paper will put to rest the objection that accurate land assessment is impracticable or inordinately difficult. Land assessment is a well-understood application of basic economic principles. Training is needed to do it at a professional level, but such training is available. Those who seek to further to the public collection of resource rents would do well to consider a career as a public assessor.

---

* When the author managed the British Columbia Assessment Authority, we were able to value 1,350,000 land parcels annually, using a land valuation computer system, which considered all land attributes, zoning, physical features and market demand factors. A multiple regression analysis system was used for the analysis of sales and testing of results.

Transport's Hidden Reward

by Dave Wetzel

Land — The Commons

For most of humankind's existence on this planet we have had to travel everywhere on foot. The early migrations from Africa to the Middle East and beyond all took place on foot.

The use of trees to create rafts, canoes and later boats to cross and navigate rivers, lakes and coastal areas were probably our first release from pedestrian travel.

When the first caveman or cavewoman used a rolling log to shift a load much heavier than they could carry, they would not have known that they were taking the first tentative steps towards an invention that would revolutionise mankind's existence on this planet.

Not only has the wheel enabled draft animals to pull carts more efficiently than they could drag loads but without it we would not have railways, cycles, automobiles and even turbines for jet engines, electric motors or indeed electricity generating stations.

Most importantly for the purpose of this paper, the wheel has brought people and places closer together.

When a village is better connected to a town by a bridge, new road or railway, both places benefit. The villagers gain access to jobs, goods and services that otherwise might not be available at all or very expensive to provide. People in the town may wish to visit the village for leisure activities (the village pub, a unique restaurant or country pursuits). New residents may be attracted to the village in order to commute daily into the town. Similarly businesses in both the town and the village acquire new customers (reducing their unit costs) and a wider pool from which to recruit staff.

Everybody benefits. Workers have new opportunities and business people make more profits. But that is only the beginning of the story as the desire to locate in both the town and the village will rise. With this increased demand for space in both the town and the village the owners of land are able to increase their rents and hence the selling price of their land. This means that landowners gain an unearned benefit from the new opportunities that the improved transport creates.

So questions arise: Why do we not mobilise unearned land values to finance transport costs? What mechanism could best be employed to achieve this?

The reality of improved transport in areas that can benefit from it is that land values (usually expressed as location values) rise in proportion to the benefits people derive from the improved transport itself. But it is not just new transport provision that creates land values, because existing transport provision also bestows a benefit to the community that landowners collect in the form of unearned wealth. Imagine any town that you know losing all its transport provision. No railway; no airport; no buses; no inter-city coaches; no trams; no petrol stations; no car repair facilities; no road repairs; no street lighting; no traffic law enforcement and no hospitals to treat victims of road crashes. What do you think would happen to the land values in such a town?

Of course, it is not only transport that gives land its value. Most public and private services in the vicinity of a site add to the desirability of the location; landowners are able to collect this benefit for themselves even though it is the whole community that creates it.

The rent of hired tools, cars or any person-made products is a reasonable payment to an entrepreneur for the cost of providing a service, a return on the savings invested and a profit that competition ensures is kept to a reasonable minimum. However, when renting a building one is effectively paying two rents. Firstly the rent of the building, for which the owner rightly expects a return on their effort in providing the building and which is approximately the same per square foot for any building wherever it is located.* The

---

* Per-square-foot building costs vary only by the quality of the building, the

second rent is a payment for the location of the building and this varies wildly, depending upon many factors: the natural environment, planning requirements, access to external services provided by both taxpayers (fire, police, education, health etc) and entrepreneurs (local shops, restaurants, bars, petrol stations, car sales and repair facilities etc.) the availability of employment and the size, skill levels, incomes and abilities of the local population — as well as transport facilities. The latter rent is described as "locational rent" or "economic rent."

In a society where land is often exchanged and bartered we seldom consider its very nature. We are all totally dependent upon it for our very existence. Apart from negligible changes arising from drainage or flood prevention the size of the land area of our planet is a fixed quantity. Ancient humans (Homo Erectus) evolved about 2 million years ago and our own species, Homo Sapiens, about 200,000 years ago. For most of this time the land was a shared bounty. Our ancestors were hunter-gatherers who paid no rent to anybody. It was not until about 10,000 years ago that agriculture developed and the early farmers who sowed the land wanted security of tenure in order to be sure that they and their family were able to reap the harvest they had sown.

Of course, private ownership of land did not materialise immediately. There were originally other forms of tenure mainly based on tribal or communal ownership. Even in Britain the Crown, on behalf of the people, is still the legal owner of all land in the UK and freeholders and leaseholders are ultimately tenants of the Crown. The idea that freeholders enjoyed rent-free occupation of their land began to be developed with the Magna Carta when the Barons used their military and political might to obtain the King's signature to enable them to stop paying their land rent — mostly in the form of services to the crown and the people. The effect of this privatisation of land has created many of the economic problems and distortions we face today. The surplus value of land that could finance our public services; this revenue could replace all the damaging taxes on people who work, produce and trade.

---

distance the materials have to be brought, slight regional differences in workers' pay and the additional services provided by the owner.

Trade and Transport

One of the distinctions between mankind and the animal kingdom is our ability to trade with one another. One person's surplus item may be of value to another who not only requires it but also has a different surplus item to offer in exchange. In this bartering situation both benefit. For each of them the item they acquire is of more value to them than the one they part with. This form of direct barter soon led to more complex ways of trading over much larger distances but however complex today, trades only take place when each party to the trade can derive a direct benefit.

Obviously international laws are required to prevent exploitation of workers (including prohibiting child labour, slavery, etc.) and the sale of unsafe products (illegal drugs, toys with poisonous paint, etc.) but generally unhindered trade should be encouraged by not having financial trade barriers either between borders (duties and tariffs) or even within a single country (VAT, or sales taxes of any kind). Customs duties and tariffs create the impression that the owners and workers in a particular industry are protected from loss of business in the short term but in reality can only damage trade and thus make everybody in the country poorer.

Of course to effect this trade a means of transport was required. Originally boats and beasts of burden were utilised and towns and communities grew around ports or staging posts along, for example, the Silk Road.

Today we see higher land values in a town with a successful port, airport and/or good road and/or rail connections. The landowners in these towns should be giving back their unearned benefit to pay for the essential services that are otherwise paid for by a tax on productive activity or trade, taxes that increase the price of goods and reduce take-home pay thus leading to unemployment and poverty.

Land Value Capture (LVC)

Land Value Capture is the generic term that refers to the different ways that increases in land value created by new transport infrastructure and services can be utilised to finance them.

Some of these methods (such as development land taxes or betterment levies) can actually be damaging to an economy whilst others are very limited both in scope and their financial advantage.

The best form of land value capture is undoubtedly an Annual Land Value Tax (LVT) whereby all the land in a jurisdiction is valued for its annual rental value according to each site's optimum permitted use. "Optimum" in terms of how the market would best like to use the site to maximise its earnings potential and "permitted" in terms of how the community, through its democratic planning processes, decides the preferred use of the site, whether it be for commerce, business, retail, residential, agriculture, leisure, open space or even kept in its natural state perhaps as a wilderness.

Previous Experience of Land Value Capture

Hong Kong is an excellent example of how land value capture can be used to provide transport and other public services. The British acquired Hong Kong as the spoils of the first Opium War in 1841 and proceeded to lease land for rent rather than sell freeholds. The consequence is that the government of Hong Kong still collects land rent today to fund public services, meaning the population and businesses enjoy low taxes on incomes and no sales taxes at all. Hong Kong built a new airport and a new subway system with funds from land values. Andrew Purves describes this phenomenon in his recent book.*

In Britain in the 19th Century the Metropolitan Underground Railway was extended from Central London to Buckinghamshire. The Government gave the railway company powers to purchase land in the catchment area of the new stations at agricultural prices which once the trains were operating they were able to sell to house builders at inflated prices. This "windfall" revenue met the cost of building the railway. However, had ownership been retained and the land leased instead of sold, the railway would have benefited from the continuing rising land values that the railway itself continues to create. This flow of income could provide funds for modernisation, well-paid staff and more reasonable fares for passengers. It would be difficult for any railway company today to own thousands of leasehold homes — so the modern approach should be for the government to introduce an annual land value tax so that all

---

* See Purves, *No Debt; High Growth; Low Tax — Hong Kong's Economic Miracle Explained*

landowners contribute to the cost of the public services that provide them with their unearned wealth.

In London many developers, when seeking planning permission, do make some contributions towards new transport infrastructure but this is very small in comparison to the landowners' gain. When I was Chair of the Greater London Council's Transport Committee in 1981 we wanted to build the Docklands Light Railway (DLR) but the Conservative Government under Mrs Thatcher would not allow us to tap into the land value gain we knew the railway would create. Consequently it was built on a very tight cash capped budget financed by taxpayers from across the country, who would not receive the cash benefits to be enjoyed by the landowners within the catchment area and most of whom would never enjoy the benefit of travelling on the railway itself.

The M25 and Road Pricing

The M25 is an orbital motorway road that circumnavigates London with a radius of about 15 miles. When it was first proposed a few enlightened people suggested that it should be financed by annual Land Value Tax. This proposal was rejected out of hand. Nevertheless, as soon as the lines were drawn on the map land values began to rise, especially for sites close to the new road junctions.

Even if LVT is too radical for a conservative government (a little "c" as both Labour and Conservative government are very conservative when it comes to consider LVT) at least road pricing should be considered as an efficient method to fund road safety, facilities for cyclists and pedestrians, genuine road improvements, bus priority measures, maintenance and traffic policing. Ken Livingstone bravely introduced congestion charging for vehicles entering central London despite massive hostility from political opponents and the media. The congestion charge has been a huge success in reducing vehicle journeys in London but it is now 14 years old. Technology has moved on and London needs a new more modern scheme that covers more hours and weekends, differentiates congested streets from free-flowing ones and charges on a mileage basis rather than one flat fee allowing unlimited access throughout the zone for a whole day.

Similarly, all major roads and motorways in the UK should

have electronic tolls that would reduce congestion, speed up essential journeys and encourage some motorists to switch to public transport.

Jubilee Line Extension (JLE)

In December 1999, at a cost of £3.5 billion, the extension to the Jubilee Line was opened from Regents Park to Stratford in East London (later to serve the site of the 2012 Olympic Park). Thanks to research by property developer Don Riley described in his book *Taken for a Ride* we know that the land values within a thousand yards around the new stations rose by a total of £13 billion – over three times the cost of building the line. At my suggestion Transport for London (TfL) appointed property consultants Jones, Lang La Salle to estimate the land value increase around two stations (Canary Wharf and Southwark) just arising from the new railway. They reported an increase of £2.8 billion from 1992, when the construction was finally agreed and 2002, two years after the trains were running.

Some academics try to measure land value uplift by comparing the value after one year of operation with the value immediately before the trains commenced service. This of course misses a huge component of the uplift as speculators and wise investors start purchasing land and property as soon as there is talk of a new line being built and certainly once the scheme has been given full approval, often a period of many years if not even decades.

This was clearly stated back in 1938 when my predecessor, Frank Pick, Vice-Chairman of London Transport gave evidence to the UK Parliament's Barlow Commission when he said

> *The moment an Underground extension is projected, the value of the land is at least doubled. When the railway is built and the stations are opened, the land adjacent to the stations is at least quadrupled in value. There is every reason, in the interests of the public, why the London Transport Passenger Board should receive its appropriate share of the land values it helps to create.*

Crossrail (The Elizabeth Line)

Crossrail is a £14.8bn 100km railway that will cross London on an east-west axis, linking the suburbs, Canary Wharf and the docklands business hub, The City of London (the square mile financial centre), West End shops, major main line stations, Heathrow Airport with towns in Middlesex, Essex and Berkshire. Serving 40 stations Crossrail is due to start operations in late 2018 when it will be carrying 200 million passengers a year.

Originally TfL wanted to finance Crossrail by means of annual Land Value Tax. When the Labour government dismissed this, an American Tax Incremental Finance scheme was proposed but was also rejected.

Since the 17th Century the UK has had a local government business property tax based on the rental values of commercial buildings. Consequently TfL together with the Ken Livingstone, the Labour Mayor proposed a new funding mechanism based on the more valuable commercial buildings within the London political administrative area, the Greater London Authority (GLA). A Crossrail Business Rate Supplement (BRS) levying 2p in the pound to raise £4.1bn capital plus interest over a period of up 30 years.

Business organisations were united in supporting the BRS proposal as presumably they anticipated the greater increase in land values that Crossrail would create.

The Treasury were very reluctant to agree to such a huge project for London but a former senior government adviser recently told me that TfL's proposal for the BRS was the game-changer that won the government's approval for the scheme.

Consequently, the Parliamentary Bill went through with no major opposition and the Business Rate Supplement has never been an election issue. Indeed when the Labour Mayor, Ken Livingstone lost an election in 2008, Boris Johnson the new Conservative Mayor (the UK's current Foreign Secretary) continued to support the BRS to part-fund Crossrail. Furthermore, in 2010 the new Conservative coalition government not only continued with the London Business Rate Supplement but also have since extended the powers to other major cities to use the same principle to fund their infrastructure plans.

Because it collects a surplus, the BRS is in effect a mini land value tax falling on a few valuable sites in London. Restricting the BRS to the more valuable business properties helped to ensure that homeowners and small businesses would not lobby against the scheme.

However, the Business Rate Supplement is not perfect by any means. Many landowners will enjoy the financial benefits of Crossrail but make no contribution through the BRS. These will include all landowners outside of the GLA area but within the catchment area of the Crossrail stations, the owners of the 80% of smaller business premises in London, all residential landowners and of course the owners of empty development and agricultural fields who have never paid any business rates.

Planners Need to Learn the Law of Rent

All environmental planners and especially transport planners need to understand the land market. During my many years in local government dating back to 1964 I have seen on several occasions sites, or parts of sites, purchased by local authorities for road, bus or rail schemes where a knowledgeable negotiator should have been able to acquire the land for nothing.

Let one example suffice. Victoria Underground station in central London is often so overcrowded that for safety reasons the staff has had to close the station to allow the trains to clear the platforms before more passengers could be let in. The station was due for modernisation and so a more expensive scheme was developed with an additional new entrance connected by a new pedestrian tunnel crossing under a major road to a shopping centre on the other side. The planners paid the shopping mall for a shop premises to accommodate the new entrance. However, had they negotiated, the owner would have willingly provided the shop for free as the Underground entrance will bring much extra trade and so all the rents in the mall will be increased.

Aviation

The highest price paid for a pair of take-off and landing slots at Heathrow Airport was $75m, paid by Oman Air to Air France-KLM for a prized early morning arrival, reported in February 2016. A year before, American Airlines paid $60m to Scandinavian Airlines.

Why should Air France-KLM "own" a landing slot that they

can sell to Oman Air for $75m? Do they own the sky? Fred Harrison discusses this subject in his book *Wheels of Fortune*.

A landing slot is a permission to occupy a particular place in the sky at a certain time. To my knowledge, no airline has created either time or space.

It seems obvious to me that these landing slots should be rented by the government to the airlines on a bidding basis. Similar to the way that 3G mobile phone companies bid for their part of the UK spectrum which raised £22.4bn in 2000 and will be re-let in 2020. The revenue collected could be used to improve public transport to the airport (reducing traffic congestion and pollution) and for sound insulation on local buildings affected by the planes, the airport and its road traffic.

Sadiq Khan, Labour's New London Mayor and the Future

Despite a racist campaign from the Conservative Party, Sadiq Khan, a Muslim son of a London bus driver, was elected Mayor in 2016.

There have been some interesting developments regarding annual Land Value Tax. In late 2015 the GLA Planning Committee adopted an all-party report suggesting a trial project for LVT in London. This has been included by the Mayor in the consultation for a new business district.

So who knows? We may yet see a successful trial of LVT completed in London and our Mayor lobbying for parliamentary powers to introduce a local Land Value Tax for Greater London in the same way that in 1938 his predecessor Herbert Morrison, the Leader of the then London County Council, put forward a Private Members Bill in Parliament calling for the Site Value Rating for London.

Introducing Land Value Taxation at the Municipal Level

by Josh Vincent

Henry George was rather silent on the specifics of implementing his "sovereign remedy." This paper describes the contemporary status of what came to be called the "Land Value Tax," (LVT). We will discuss the political, administrative, and technical issues involved in introducing, implementing and administering the reform. LVT must be shown to be practical in the modern context of government. Part of this challenge is to show that it can deliver benefits that make it worth the political effort.

The LVT reform offered to minicipalites today is a descendent of the "Single Tax Limited," which was first proposed in the late 1880s by Thomas Shearman, a close associate of Henry George. This policy, though ambitious, is much less overarching than the full collection of economic rent. Proposed as a fiscal reform, this strategy offers a mechanism by which the economic rent of land can be collected through the existing tax system, while gradually reducing or eliminating other forms of taxation.

Since the 1910s, this form of land value taxation has been demonstrated to be operable at several levels of government. It is scalable, and delivers outcomes that are replicable and well-documented. Outcomes can be measured from such prosaic evidence as a change in a homeowner's annual tax bill, to aggregate data indicating economic growth, reversal of economic decline, and better use of community created infrastructure and value.

LVT must be understood as a bridge between fiscal reform and a blueprint for a better society. While it is implemented through a gradual shift of property tax rates, LVT's potential significance is much greater. It can quickly be deployed as a powerful tool to undo centuries of deadweight loss that retards personal and community benefit and prosperity.

Brief history — Pittsburgh and Scranton

Our story begins in Pittsburgh, Pennsylvania in the early part of the 20th century. Civic-minded progressives took steps to modernize Pittsburgh's government and community. Several tax reforms were enacted. These included the equalization of property assessments, the exemption of personal machinery from taxation, and the citywide unification of school district tax rates. In 1913, respected organizations outside of city government began recommending a version of land value tax that would impose half the mill rate (property tax rate per $1,000 of assessed value) on buildings as on land values.

Many organizations supported this "Graded Tax" plan. Among them were the Pittsburgh Real Estate Board, Single Tax Club of Pittsburgh, the Pittsburgh Civic Commission, the Pittsburgh Board of Trade and the Civic Club of Allegheny County. The law was implemented in 1914 (also including the only other City of the Second Class in Pennsylvania, Scranton in the Northeast).[*] The original property tax had been .89%. In the first year it was replaced with a tax rate of .94% on land values and .846% on building values.

Graded Tax Spreads to Smaller Communities

Eventually, municipalities and various smaller cities in Pennsylvania started to ask the state for the same right enact LVT for municipal purposes. In 1951, cities of the Third Class were allowed to adopt LVT.[†]

---

[*] Under state law, Pennsylvania has four classes of cities, divided by population: First Class, one million or more (Philadelphia is the only one); Second Class, 80,000 to 999,999 (Second class A is less than 250K); Third Class, cities with fewer that 250,000 people who have not elected to become part of Second Class A.

[†] Act. No. 299, incorporated into Senate Bill 357, dealt with taxation and assessment of land and improvements. Thereafter, Public Law 37531 allowed Third Class cities to adopt LVT.

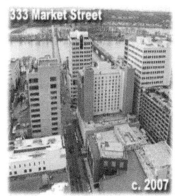

LVT played a key role in turning around the economy of Pennsylvania's capital city of Harrisburg

Pennsylvania also has a plethora of smaller communities called boroughs. Many boroughs had shown interest in LVT since the 1951 bill, but movement did not take place until the late 1990s. With the sturdy support of Alanna Hartzok's Earthrights Institute in Chambersburg, Senator Terry Punt's 1997 SB 211 extended the LVT option to the nearly 1,000 Pennsylvania boroughs; the bill was signed into law by Governor Thomas Ridge in 1998. This legislation was supported by the Pennsylvania State Association of Boroughs.

School Districts

A further limiting factor to the scope of Pennsylvania's graded tax is the fact that school districts are their own taxing jurisdictions. This was addressed somewhat by Act 16 in 1993, allowing school districts coterminous with Third Class cities to levy higher rates of taxation on assessed land values. Eight districts qualify under this law.

Home Rule

The Home Rule Charter and Optional Plans Law grants Pennsylvania municipalities the power to determine for themselves what structure their government will have and what services it will perform. A home rule municipality drafts and amends its own charter and can exercise any powers or functions not denied by the state Constitution or the General Assembly. As of 2006, 71 municipalities have adopted home rule charters, including 6 counties, 19 cities, 19 boroughs and 27 townships. Home Rule is crucial to furtherance of LVT, especially in relation to the city of Philadelphia.

Currently, thirteen cities, two school districts, and the Pittsburgh Downtown improvement District deploy LVT.

Elsewhere in the US

LVT was enacted by the state of Hawaii, but the state government abolished it in 1977.

Two "Single Tax communities" have been established, in Arden, Delaware and Fairhope, Alabama.

State law permitting LVT is the next Rubicon for the rest of the country. Maryland, Virginia, Connecticut, and New York have statutes that would permit LVT for local governments (or even at the state level in Maryland).

Does your town need LVT?

There are several approaches when broaching the idea of LVT to a community. There has to be a reason to explore LVT: advocates must identify real problems that the proposed reform will solve.

Current tax systems in most communities are based upon three types of taxation: wages, sales and commerce, and property. Property taxes make up a plurality of the city's revenue, with some exceptions — but reliance on property taxation has been declining in many communities.

In many cases, a city that is in decline can be the most obvious candidate for LVT. A declining city will have lost much of its tax base. A perfect example would be a postindustrial city along the lines of Detroit, St. Louis, or Hartford. Before the 1950s, such cities had a balanced tax base of industrial, commercial, and residential real estate. But, both the industrial base and capital-intensive commercial developments have severely declined.

Along with the decline of the tax base often comes the emigration of a well-educated and community-minded middle-class. Traditionally the guarantor of good schools and various other public services, the middle class provided a shield for the working poor and unemployed; this helped to create an environment that wealthier people would choose to inhabit. The table shows the body-blows that cities — almost all of which are in the Northeast or the upper Midwest — have suffered since the days of peak population (generally 1950) to 2010.

Percent Decline in Population from Peak

In these declining cities, the tax penalties placed on business, wages, buildings and equipment outweigh the advantages these cities offer. Implementation of LVT helps stabilize or reverse the effects of deadweight loss that taxation imposes upon urban areas.

One could throw a dart anywhere on a map to see the economic drag and disincentives of badly constructed tax policies. Mercer County, New Jersey is a typical example. For nearly two centuries the state capital city of Trenton was the economic engine of Mercer County. Its manufacturing reputation was second to none; visitors from Pennsylvania would see a large sign on a railroad bridge announcing "Trenton Makes, the World Takes."

Today, due to the nearly complete abandonment of the city by the middle class and the wealthy, the perceived value of Trenton sites — and hence Trenton's property tax base — has cratered. Yet, the rest of Mercer County compares much more favorably, as shown in the different communities' effective property tax rates. The increasing effective rates on inner-city parcels ratchets up the disincentive effects of the tax system, creating insurmountable obstacles to development.

Except for the well-to-do borough of Hopewell (whose poverty rate hovers around zero, and whose school-district taxes are sky-high), Trenton is far and away the highest taxed jurisdiction, with an effective tax rate of just over 5% per annum. In the leafy suburbs of Mercer County, effective property tax rates are much more reasonable. The borough of Princeton is packed with expensive taxable real estate, even though nearly half of the value is exempt due to Princeton University.

With LVT, Trenton could establish a permanent universal tax abatement on buildings. It could even provide a source for forgiveness of state sales and income taxes inside city boundaries.

Pathways to Implementation

For example, we'll look at the city of Allentown, Pennsylvania. Allentown has dual tax rates: 50.38 Mills on land values and 10.72 Mills on building values: the mill rate on land is nearly five times greater than on buildings. To collect the same revenue under a standard tax, Allentown would need a rate of 17.52 Mills.

Without LVT, nearly 80% of Allentown's property tax revenue would come from what it needs most: injections of capital for building construction and maintenance. When these things are done, jobs are created, and eventually homeowners and tenants come into the city.

Without LVT, only 20% of Allentown's property tax revenue would come from land values. The value created by government investment, and by the community's people, would sit fallow — or be pocketed by speculative investors. Often, speculative investors are also absentee owners.

LVT removes incentives that reward private land banking as a viable business model. Municipalities must get the most "bang for the buck" from land that is on the tax rolls. Taxing land value provides permanent incentives for growth and reinvestment that go beyond temporary and targeted tax incentives. And taxing land value can serve as a partial or full replacement of other taxes known to be economically corrosive (i.e. sales, business, or income tax).

It is well recognized that the current property tax creates a powerful disincentive for strong cities and economically empowered populations. LVT is designed to reverse that disincentive, and to create new incentives by removing tax barriers to investment and sweat equity. LVT allows the market to incentivize Smart Growth objectives, without using the coercive powers of government.

Are there problems with local or regional LVT? Most of the known complaints and problems with a land value tax are related to the following four key issues:

Taxation of unrealized capital gains: The property tax in general is an unpopular tax, largely because it is a tax on wealth rather than current cash flow. When the parcel's value increases, the tax goes up, but the owner does not receive this benefit until the property is sold.

Land value assessment and rate setting: Land value taxation requires accurate land assessments. With a traditional property tax, the important number is the total; how it is divided between land and buildings is unimportant. With a land value tax, the division is very important. Commercial and income-producing buildings are often overvalued for the purpose if income-tax depreciation. This distortion would distort and weaken the effectiveness of LVT.

Winners and losers: Changing from a property tax to a land value tax creates winners and losers and therefore raises concerns about fairness. This can contribute to political confrontations. In general, however, the losers will be those who put relatively large land areas to relatively low-intensity uses: examples include fast-food franchises, big-box retailers and car dealerships.

Lack of understanding: Perhaps most importantly, the land value tax and its benefits are not well understood, either by public officials or citizens at large.

The overall market: At a given time, there may be little demand for new or renovated buildings, meaning that lowering the tax rate on buildings will have little effect on the amount of development. If the land value tax is adopted with the unrealistic hope of developing an area that has no market potential, the switch to a land value tax redistributes tax burdens without any efficiency gains (at least in the short term).

All towns are different; study is needed. Most towns will benefit from LVT. But, before effort is devoted to a possibly ill-advised campaign, it is wise to conduct studies to determine the potential effectiveness of any changes in tax structure. The degree of tax shift and the rate of implementation can be custom-designed for a given city's circumstances.

What is necessary for a community to accept the need for tax policy reform, and how may it be implemented? We'll focus on tactics and strategies that have worked over the past 50 years in the United States. Programmatically, these may work in other nations such as Canada and other nations that have valuations upon which to base a land value tax system.

"Thanks for inviting me to your town"

Usually the best introduction comes from somebody within the community. Now that some cities have used LVT for several decades, the reform is not entirely unheard-of. In the US, it is generally acknowledged that LVT slumbered fitfully after its enactment in the early 1900s in Pittsburgh and Scranton.

Why did smaller cities not implement LVT when they became eligible? Generally, from the 1950s to the mid-1970s, cities were fairly prosperous and comfortable. Each had its own industrial niche, and there were markets for their products at home and abroad. In the 1970s, the first wave of deindustrialization started to sting. Small manufacturing companies lost market share to newer factories and plants in Asia and Germany. The steel industry, long a symbol of American industrial might and prosperity, began to wither in the face of international competition, and lack of capital investments in existing steel plants.

At the same time, LVT proponents were in transition. The Georgist economic remedy — otherwise known as the "Single Tax" or LVT — had the support of union members and small business people, but its influence faded. Other forms of taxation crowded onto the scene: income, sales, and business taxes.

In the 1970s, Dr. Steven Cord, a professor at Indiana University of Pennsylvania, joined members of the Henry George Foundation of America on visits to cities in Western Pennsylvania. There he would observe groups of Council people or Rotary Club breakfast attendees. Dr. Cord went about convicing such groups that the rising crisis demanded alternatives to business as usual. He devised a formula that any city treasurer or controller could employ to understand and predict the effects of applying various degrees of LVT. With some tinkering over the years, this is the formula still used today to research LVT, issue tax bills and adopt budgets.

How to do it

In the appendix, we'll employ Dr. Cord's formula for repairing the property tax, using numbers for an actual city and its tax base, so that less revenue flows from buildings and more from land value. This is generally known as "Two-Rate." Basically, a chosen rate of reduction in the tax rate on buildings would require that revenue loss be made up by a calculated increase in the tax rate on land values.

The intent of two-rate LVT is to apply disincentives to blight and vacancy and remove disincentives for investment and sweat equity. The cost of holding a vacant, blighted, or bare lot is increased. Also, when the tax on buildings is lowered, the cost of labor and the expenditure of capital in constructing and maintaining a building is reduced. Buildings that had been unprofitable to construct can now become viable under the new tax system.

A higher tax on land value heavily incentivizes vacant land into better use. Also, land ownership is strongly correlated with income. A shift to LVT tends to create a more progressive property tax.

What are the alternatives?

Looming issues of tax inequality and regressivity have increased since the recession of 2008. Cities and states have a great need to make the property tax progressive and to provide stable revenue. The current property tax provides stable revenue, to some extent — but it is widely criticized for its perceived regressivity. LVT delivers both stability and progressivity.

In particular, tax incidence has increased on lower earners. Cities and states have become reluctant to increase the property tax, due to its peculiar unpopularity. Governments have turned instead to taxation on incomes, especially high wage incomes, in states like California, Connecticut, New Jersey and New York. Of course, the wealthy have learned not to collect their wealth in wages, but to use shelters, deductions and very good lawyers. The State of New Jersey learned, to its chagrin, that the wealthiest man in New Jersey — a hedge fund manager — decided to bail on New Jersey's top income tax rate of 8.97%, actually threatening a significant hole in New Jersey's budget. He now resides in income tax-free Florida.

Another unfortunate tax option is hidden and regressive: sales and excise taxes, which have become very popular with cash-strapped local and state governments. Economists and poor folk agree that the sales tax is a lousy choice. In particular local sales taxes treat poor communities very harshly.

In 2016 Philadelphia imposed a highly regressive tax on sugary drinks, popularly called the "soda tax," of about 3¢ an ounce. Most consumption of sweetened drinks are in lower-income areas. If we were to make the conservative assumption that one household might drink four liters of soda per week, the added tax burden of 3¢ per ounce comes to $212 a year. That's respectively the equivalent of 9% of the median annual property tax for a residential parcel in Philadelphia. Yet, it was the fear of increasing the property tax that made this highly regressive tax politically feasible!

True Tax progressivity with AXI

We referred, above, to the frequently inaccurate allocations of land and building values in local assessments. In many areas, this inaccuracy, along with the overall volatility of real estate markets, can mean that simply applying the standard two-rate formula would mean higher tax bills for most homeowners — which is neither economically nor politically to be desired. To find a way to bring the benefits of LVT to such areas, the Center for the Study of Economics has developed an alternative method: the Assessment Exemption on Improvements (AXI). A blanket permanent abatement of a certain dollar amount on buildings is put into effect (for example, the median value of a house, not counting land, in that area). The overall tax rate then rises accordingly, yielding a revenue-neutral shift with a greater impact on land value. For example, if someone's building is worth $50,000 and the AXI is $50,000 then they will pay no tax on the building. If the building is worth $500,000 then the owner would pay tax on $450,000 of the building value.

This can have the effect of dramatically reducing tax burden on lower-valued parcels, most often residences, but also "mom and pop businesses" and mixed-use parcels. By employing this technique, we can devise an LVT reform that would provide immediate and substantial tax relief to homeowners, from poor to upper middle class, while maintaining or enhancing revenue flows. By that measure, it is a model with much vertical equity.

AXI shifts the tax burden to those properties with either the ability to pay, or the capacity to build and profit from what is now fallow land.

Appendix

How is Two-Rate Determined?

Calculating the land tax rate (LTRp) when the building tax rate (BTRp) is known: First obtain the citywide building assessments (BA) and land assessments (LA).

Calculate the rates that will yield the same revenue for the city as the current property tax rate, with a 20% reduction in building tax:

$$LTRp = (PTRc - BTRp) \times BA/LA + PTRc$$

Now to continue the exercise, we will replace the language with a real city in trouble; one discussed earlier in this chapter: Trenton New Jersey:

$$.0856692 = (0.05005-0.04004)*3.55836+0.05005$$

Therefore, to start the process of LVT, Trenton would reduce its tax on buildings from 5.005% to 4.004% and increase the tax rate on land values to 8.56692%.

Please note that these LVT rates will raise the same revenue as the flat rate. Very few jurisdictions want to reduce revenues, or increase revenue when introducing a new tax. That's political reality: in out years, shifts can be made to increase revenue. In Trenton, for example, the property tax with or without an emphasis on buildings will still bring in approximately $100 million year, using these effective (not statutory) tax rates.

How is AXI Determined?

First a number is chosen that fits the dataset. For a model, the goal would the median value of all taxable buildings in the city (for example, in 2015, in the city of Bridgeport, CT, that was $48,640). This example uses Bridgeport because it is distressed, and has the highest effective property tax rate in the nation — which falls generally upon low value homes owned by low wage earners.

First each property must be credited with the AXI, then the formula can be used:

a. (BAi-$48,640, MAX $0) = New BAi c
b. New BAi + Lai = New total assessment
c. Sum all properties for a Grand Total:
(LA $2,490,402,837+New BA $$3,125,392,851)=
$5,615,795,688
d. PTRp = $294,500,000/$5,615,795,688
      (Revenue divided by Assessments = Rate)
e. PTRp = 52.441367mills

Community Land Trusts as a Strategy for Community Collection of Economic Rent

by Gary Flomenhoft

"You never change things by fighting the existing reality. To change something, build a new model that makes the existing model obsolete." — R. Buckminster Fuller

Introduction

Community Land Trusts (CLTs) have been an alternative strategy for prevention of private rent-seeking since they were created in 1969. Today, there are some 250 CLTs in the United States. Recently, a huge surge of interest has developed in the United Kingdom, which now has 170 CLTs since 2008. This new interest, in owner-occupied housing with limited financial returns, is a reaction to the failure of housing policy in the US and UK. The housing bubble and financial collapse of 2008 led to the Global Financial Crisis (GFC) — but it generated no effective reform. Housing prices again inflated to levels median income earners could not afford, in many countries including the US, UK, and Australia.

This essay will discuss the potential of Community Land Trusts (CLTs) as an alternative to the historical approach of trying to implement land value taxation, in order to capture "land rent" (unearned income) for public revenue. I will discuss difficulties of the legislative approach, explain the alternative of Community Land Trusts including legal structures, respond to critiques, provide a status of CLTs around the world, and explain the benefits to Georgists of their involvement.

Georgist History: Success and Failure

The Georgist movement in its heyday had a huge impact on public policy and professional practices, including valuing land and buildings separately, and the enduring impact of site value (land only) taxes in Australia and New Zealand instead of taxing "capital improvement value" (land and buildings combined) in many jurisdictions. Australia collects land taxes at the state level and many local council rates (property taxes) use the site value only method. However, this has done nothing to make housing affordable. Home prices in Australia have reached absurd levels of over 7 times average annual income, reaching $660,000 nationally in 2015 and $995,804 in Sydney in 2016.

Collection of economic rent through royalties and severance taxes on minerals is another successful implementation of Georgist principles worldwide. But the promise of Henry George's "tax" on economic rent is largely unfulfilled. This is especially true in the realm of real estate, which comprises the largest asset in any society. Progress is stalled. Rentiers have been making a comeback through the neo-liberal political dominance since the Reagan/Thatcher revolution of the 1980s. The dominant philosophy worldwide is now privatization of the commons, debt peonage to banks, and austerity for everyone else. John Warnock explains the terms liberal vs. democratic theory of rent:

> The democratic theory of rent suggests that governments should maximize their collection of rent to the benefit of their publics, who own the resources. The liberal theory of rent suggests that public resources should be privatized and employed to make profits, and that rents should remain in private hands either entirely, or enough to ensure investment in the industry. (Warnock, 2006, page 6)

Clearly the liberal theory of rent is currently winning, as shown by the 2008 land bubble and the renewal of the land cycle after the crash, with no mitigating policies put into place. Efforts to influence taxation policy by Georgists should certainly continue, but other strategies should also be considered. They are not mutually exclusive, but complementary.

Difficulties of the Political Approach

In the late 1800s landowners may have been the primary rentiers, but that role has been taken over by the banks and the financial sector, who own 50% of real estate equity. In Australia homeowners have about 48% of the equity in their homes; in the US they have about 54%. In the US, the GI bill and easy credit have contributed to a state of affairs in which 67% of housing is owner-occupied. That leaves only 33% of housing owned by landlords, speculators, and investors, in the traditional senses of those terms. Banks have an incentive for prices to rise as high as possible: the higher the price, the more interest they make. Land prices are inflated in a self-reinforcing process, because both mortgage lenders and property owners benefit from higher prices.

It is well known that property developers have a huge influence on local and municipal government, perhaps even the dominant influence in many places. But the linchpin of control by the land rentiers is the homeowners themselves. According to Saul Eslake, eight million Australians are property owners, and only 100,000 purchase property each year. Therefore the constituency for rising land prices outnumbers the constituency for affordable housing by eighty to one. It is therefore not surprising the property lobby prevails in public policy. Homeowners have been turned into allies of the speculators and rentiers, and have become rentiers themselves. This makes the political approach very difficult.

Reversal of Progress

Even if progress is made towards collection of economic rent, a succeeding government can reverse the policy, and all its public benefits. This was seen in Pittsburgh when the split rate tax, in effect since 1913, was reversed in 2001.

This may also describe what happened to the Justice Party in Denmark in 1960 after joining the ruling coalition from 1957-1960. The Danish Georgist economist Knud Tholstrup wrote,

> In 1957 the Justice Party, together with the Social Democrats (Labour) and the Radical Left Wing Party (Liberals actually) formed what was to become the most prosperous ever Danish Government — later termed the Ground Rent Government... three years in

power, Denmark had no foreign debt, no inflation and an unemployment level of 1%, considered full employment. So why is this not continuing?... the general election of 1960, the opposition used, for the time, the largest sum ever in any Danish election campaign, financed by the Conservatives and Landowner associations... against the site revenue legislation continued after the election and the new, weakened government gave in. Further strong pressure from land-owner associations had the site revenue laws repealed in 1964.

This may be the Achilles heel of the political approach to Georgist reform: the opposition has the financial resources to reverse legislation detrimental to their real estate interests.

What happened? "Prior to 1960, 'Georgist' beliefs dictated that when a heavy "tax" is levied upon land value, land price will decrease. The consequences of full employment, no inflation, no foreign debt, increasing production and rising real wages however, brought about a prodigious demand for homes, enterprises and of course land. Land prices did not initially fall, as was predicted. In fact land prices rose. The Justice Party was unprepared for this."

Georgists tended to believe in Henry George's analysis which predicted that heavy taxation of land rent would cause land prices to fall, and that full public collection of land rent would make land prices disappear. This theoretical point has not been disproved. However, it has become apparent that a relatively light tax on land rent can indeed stimulate increased land prices.[*]

Examples of Bottom-up Change

Another strategy is to demonstrate the principle by creating an alternative model on a smaller scale. It may be argued that all political change starts at the grassroots level and percolates up from there. Some recent examples include charter schools, cigarette bans, medical marijuana, gay marriage, etc. All started as local initiatives and became national as they had a strong constituency. The main constituency regarding land reform is against it! Efforts to obtain land value taxation (LVT) at the local level only succeed when it can be demonstrated that a major-

---

[*] See Alanna Hartzok on The Alaska Permanent Fund on page 91

ity of voters would personally benefit. It is hoped that a critical mass will be obtained and the policy can be taken to the next level and expanded to other resources besides local real estate.

Community Land Trusts as Georgist Reform

Georgists should be willing to consider other possible tactics and strategies. The concept of the Community Land Trust (CLT) has a 100% Georgist pedigree. It does not exclude the political approach, but might in fact be conducive to it. Community Land Trusts were created due to the efforts of several Georgists in the US in the 1960s and 70s including Ralph Borsodi, Mildred Loomis, Robert Swann, and others. John Emmeus Davis, the leading promoter of CLTs in the US, covers their Georgist origins in an excellent presentation on "Roots of the CLT" on his website.[†]

Community Land Trusts are not-for-profit organizations comprised of property owners, residents, financiers, and NGO representatives who choose to carve out a section of town or distributed properties, where land appreciation accrues to the community and not to homeowners. The primary service is the provision of permanently affordable housing or other assets, which is accomplished by preventing the accumulation of the "unearned increment" (capital gains) in the hands of property owners. A CLT is set up by the community and for the community. The members of the CLT control it and the assets can only be sold or developed in a manner that benefits the local community. If the CLT decides to sell the asset, the cash realised is protected by an asset lock and is re-invested into something else that the trust's members think will benefit the local community. Any profits generated by the CLT cannot be paid by way of dividend or otherwise to its members but must be used to further the community's interests.

CLTs have an open democratic structure. People who live and work in the defined local community, including occupiers of the real estate that the CLT owns, must have the opportunity to become members of the CLT. The CLT should actively engage members of the community in its work and ensure that they remain engaged in the development and operation of the CLT. A CLT does not disappear when a home is sold or let but has a long-term

---

† https://www.youtube.com/watch?v=aC7YRbih4IY

role in stewarding the homes. In some cases they will remain the landlord of the rental homes or will retain an element of unsold equity in the homes. At the least, the CLT will retain the freehold.

This is the Georgist ideal in miniature. Many Georgists are critical of enclaves, citing Arden (Delaware) or Fairhope (Alabama), where higher LVT has been stymied and economic rent is still kept mostly by landowners. The major advantage of CLTs is that homeowners' share of returns (capital gains) is limited by deed, and deeds are "in perpetuity." Unlike tax legislation, these deeds cannot be reversed, and they are permanent. Land within the CLT is legally eliminated as a market commodity; there is no need to rely on taxation to claw back economic rent. The rent-seeking urge may just be too strong for homeowners and property developers to withstand, and politicians can always be influenced.

Permanence and Risk of Community Land Trusts

Community Land Trust contracts cannot be overturned or reversed as easily as legislation. I know of no case where this has happened since Community Land Trusts were created by Robert Swann in 1969. This is a major strength of CLTs. Rob Leuchs, manager of the shared equity program at the Champlain Housing Trust, informed me that in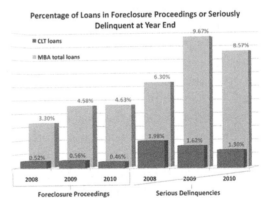
the 32 years of the land trust, they lost only two homes back to the regular housing market due to defaults, foreclosures, or poor maintenance leaving the property in bad condition. The default and foreclosure rate for CLTs is in fact only 10% of the rate for market-rate housing).

CLT Organization

Instead of a municipality collecting economic rent through

property taxation, the Community Land Trust collects a monthly lease fee, and economic rent upon sale of the property. The CLT receives the primary share of the capital gain on the property, while the homeowner's share is limited by the deed, often to the increase in the CPI, or a figure like 25% at the highest. In the "classic" CLT, the trust owns the land itself and the homeowner owns the building. Another arrangement is for the CLT and homeowner to share the equity in cases where the land and building cannot be divided (such as Australia or New Zealand). That is legally the case for condominiums, and is often easier for other kinds of real estate, especially if the land trust is distributed throughout the municipality. In these cases the CLT and homeowner share equity, and the property is valued, assessed, bought and sold just like all other surrounding property.

Shared equity is the main program for the largest CLT in the world, the Champlain Housing Trust in Burlington, Vermont. Founded in 1984, it has 2,200 apartments, and 565 owner-occupied homes distributed across three counties in Vermont. From the point of view of neighbors or the community, there is no visible difference between land trust property and the surrounding properties. There is also little or no difference from the standpoint of the bank, as the homeowner has a regular mortgage — albeit subsidized by the CLT. The invisible difference is that the homeowner is not able to pocket a capital gain upon sale of the property. The return to the homeowner is limited by the deed. The homeowner receives a subsidy from the CLT upon purchase of the property, which is approximately equivalent to the land value. The CLT owns a "ground lease" to the land, so in actuality the homeowner is only purchasing the house, even though the house and land are not divided in the mortgage. The system of shared equity for CLTs is being pursued in Australia, because in most jurisdictions, unlike the US, land and building ownership may not be separated. The homeowner gives up the capital gain upon sale of the property, in return for a large down payment subsidy.

Champlain Housing Trust Example

An example might illustrate the principle. I have been a resident and beneficiary of the Champlain Housing Trust for 10 years.

The condominium I own and am currently selling was purchased for $155,000 in 2010. The CHT provided a down payment subsidy on the property of $50,000, so I did not have to save up a down payment, and only needed a mortgage for $105,000. My interest rate at the time was 5.1%, which is rather high right now, but refinancing costs were not worth it for the time period I planned to hold it. According to a calculator online the monthly payment for a 30 yr. mortgage at 5.1% on $155k is $841/month, and on $105k is $570. That means I am saving $271 per month or $3,257 per year. I have owned it for 6 years so have saved $19,546 so far. In return for saving money during ownership I give up capital gains later when the property is sold.

Staff at CHT have told me that some residents have still asked them why they cannot receive the capital gain upon sale! It seems that the concept of getting something for nothing is just ingrained in people, especially in real estate.

Now that I am selling the condo, I can illustrate the sale portion of the equation. The property was appraised at $167,000, an increase of $12,000 since I purchased it in 2010. The buyer agreed to purchase the property for that amount. I was not reimbursed for substantial wear and tear expenses I incurred such as a new water heater, carpet, new sink and floor, or a new furnace I have to install due to failing inspection. I am getting paid 25% of the $10,000 gain from $155,000 to $165,000, or $2500. The total reimbursement from the CLT is $4500. I paid the bank principal down from $105,000 to $94,000 or $11,000. So the total I will receive upon sale will be $4500 + $11,000 = $15,500. I paid closing costs of $5000 when I purchased the property, spent about $5000 on maintenance, and selling costs will be about $1000, making total costs of $11,000. So the actual gain is more like $15,500 - $11,000 = $4,500. But if I had been renting I would have gotten nothing back. Don't forget the $19,546 I saved along the way! Counting that, my total gain is $24,046.

A "Classic" CLT is more suitable if the CLT owns a large plot of land and is able to build a development of multiple housing, or have owner-built housing. In this case ownership of the land is retained by the CLT and housing is owned by the resident. The seven rural land trust communities of the School of Living operate this way. This is illustrated by figure two where the CLT owns the land and the homeowner owns the building and has a ground lease from the CLT, and pays a monthly lease-fee. Incidentally, this is not much different from Singapore, Hong Kong, or Canberra, Australia where the municipality owns the majority of land and leases it out. The major difference is that CLT homeowners are restricted from profiting from the sale of their leases, while lease-holders in the aforementioned cities are able to sell their leases for capital gains, resulting in astronomical real estate prices.

Financing CLTs

A CLT organization may own or purchase land like any non-profit housing developer. They may choose to develop single or multi-family housing on the property. Income qualified homeowners then obtain a regular mortgage for purchase of a home, while paying a (nominal) lease fee to

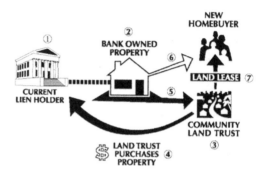

the CLT organization. One unique characteristic of CLTs is their democratic structure, where residents vote for and can serve on the board of directors of the CLT.

Shared-equity CLTs

As discussed above, there are some forms of real estate in which ownership of land and buildings cannot be legally separated. Examples include condominiums, and some jurisdictions like Australia and New Zealand. In these cases the legal structure can take the form of a shared-equity or co-ownership agreement, sometimes called

"tenants-in-common". Since land cannot be separately owned by the CLT, the resident and CLT own the entire property in common including land and buildings. When the homeowner purchases the property, the mortgage may just be for the building, or if the entire property is purchased, as is done in the Champlain Housing Trust, the CLT may provide a down payment subsidy equivalent to the value of the land portion. In this manner, the homeowner obtains a mortgage for only the value of the building, and the land portion is paid by the CLT.

Critiques of CLTs

One of the criticisms of CLTs is that they only serve low-income people, typically 80% of median income. Although most of the Champlain Housing Trust's programs are for low income people, some of them do not have any income restrictions, and if people increase their income during residency they are not disqualified. Many people consider the CLT a "stepping stone" to buying market-rate housing so they can cash in on free money like everyone else. But there is no reason CLTs could not expand into commercial property, non-profits, social services, farms, parks, multi-family, and serve people of all income levels, not just low-income residents.

Georgist Enclaves

Another critique of Community Land Trusts is that they are an enclave and only serve a small portion of the community. That is true, however many Georgist efforts have gone into lobbying for land value taxation (LVT) at the local level in the US. Every city that has LVT is an enclave in comparison to cities around them. Steven Cord has done some noteworthy comparisons of growth rates in LVT towns compared to those surrounding them, demonstrating the higher growth rates and greater number of building permits. An LVT town is a model for others. If a state adopted LVT then they would be an enclave in comparison to states around them, as Pennsylvania is to some degree. Alaska is an enclave, in that its residents receive a dividend check from economic rent (royalties) on oil, but other states and adjacent Canadian provinces do not. A CLT is just an enclave on a smaller scale. In Burlington,

Vermont, the Community Land Trust comprises 7.6 percent of the total housing stock; this has a significant impact on the housing market.*

We have to start somewhere.

CLTs Around the World

Since the Burlington, VT Community Land Trust was formed in 1984 (when Bernie Sanders was mayor), there are now about 250 CLTs in the US. According to the UK CLT Network, since they were introduced to the UK in 2006-2008, there are now 170 Community Land Trusts in UK, with half of them formed in the last two years. There is also an emerging CLT movementin Belgium, France, Italy and Australia.

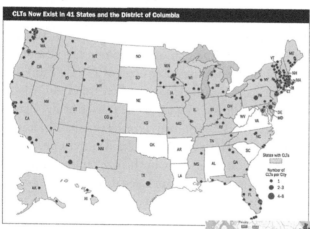

Community land trusts in the United States (chart produced by Yesim Sungyu-Eryilmaz for the National CLT Academy, 2008)

CLTs in Great Britain

---

* See Blumgart, "How Bernie Sanders Made Burlington Affordable"

What's in it for Georgists?

If Georgist organizations started creating Community Land Trusts, instead of just being lobbyists, they could provide a public service that would gain goodwill on the part of residents who benefit. Many social movements are able to advance their political agenda by providing public services. The Syriza Party in Greece is a recent example. By living in CLTs, Georgists could get on boards of these organization and influence their political agenda in favour of land value taxation and other resource-rent-for-revenue policies. Those who don't believe in private accumulation of economic rent could demonstrate their values by living in communities where they don't. Creating CLTs would give Georgists a geographical base and assets, perhaps even providing office space and other services.

Going further, Georgists could create CLT banks which would be considered Community Development Finance Institutions (CDFIs) in the US. CDFIs may enjoy numerous tax advantages and could further promote the development of CLTs. Banks are able to leverage their capital and deposits to create credit, mainly for mortgages. We could begin to reduce the power of the private banking sector by creating Community Land Trust banks, and financing Community Land Trusts. We could also help people regain sovereignty over their own lives by hiring employee-owned companies for construction, maintenance, legal, and other services. The strategy of lobbying politicians to collect economic rent instead of taxes has been pursued for over 120 years with limited success. There are alternative strategies to achieve the same goals. Community Land Trusts are one of the best.

How Should Forests Be Taxed?

By Mason Gaffney

F orest economists and entrepreneurs may think their problems are different from others', and their industry is unique. Nevertheless forest taxation can be cogently examined from the viewpoint of a general tax economist, who is interested in overall efficiency and equity in our society.

All agree that forests should be taxed on the basis of parity and equity with other industries and resources. But, with parity in respect to what? There is no substance to "parity" until we define the base. Let us survey alternative bases for taxation. We'll start with the most ridiculous, and progress toward the sublime.

The Yield Tax

The popularity of the case for yield taxation rests partly on the assumption that the rate will not be raised enough to compensate for the exemption of standing timber from the property tax. The yield tax rate has to be much higher to allow for the fact that it is collected only once every fifty years instead of once each year.

The yield tax imposes high instability on the revenues of local government revenues. They are often much smaller than the owners, especially large corporate owners, who frequently own millions of acres, and have diversified interests. These owners turn yield tax revenues on and off at their convenience.

Yield taxes are inherently biased against quick recovery of capital, because costs are not deductible. Any rate high enough to be more than a joke when applied to a long Douglas-fir cycle of, say, 80 years will also be high enough to wipe out nursery or Christmas tree farming altogether. The bias is not just against small trees, but against short investment cycles of all kinds — and against lands which respond better to intensive management practices, where timber grows faster by nature, or which is adapted to faster growing species.

A yield tax, like all local taxes, is capitalized into lower land values. This, in turn, removes the pressure to restock cutover land. There is always the alternative of letting nature restock it. This process is much slower, and leaves the land asleep like Rip Van Winkle for twenty years before it gets back to work.

The yield tax encourages substituting capital and land for labor. The less-frequent application of labor to forest land contributes its bit to the national unemployment problem, and more specifically to unemployment in sylvan areas. It is a modern reflex to disregard unemployment as a local issue, kicking it upstairs to the Feds. But the effect of institutional structure on unemployment is worth considering — and in this light the yield tax is a poor choice.

Yield taxation affords a 100% loophole for owners who never cut their stands, but use them for amenities, recreation, or nothing at all. The last is not so rare, considering all the land locked up in unsettled estates, and other dead hands.

The yield tax, in my opinion is no choice at all. The cumulative weight of the case against it is overwhelming.

The Income Tax

The income tax differs from the yield tax in that costs are deductible, which allows it to avoid the worst bite of the bias against short investment cycles and the "invisible high grading"* that is caused by a yield tax. Most land which is marginal before taxes remains marginal after taxes.

To raise the same revenue as a yield tax, the income tax must be at a substantially higher figure, at least where rotations are medium or short. This high rate leads to strenuous contortions motivated by tax avoidance. The deductibility feature leads easily to padding expenses and goldplating of capital equipment. It is harder for a tax

---

* In forestry, "high grading" is the practice of harvesting only the highest-value trees in a given area. When this is done repeatedly, it tends to degrade the overall value of timber land.

auditor to identify the goldplating of capital than to identify the consumption elements in payroll. This results in a capital-intensive bias.

The income tax as presently written is preferential towards income from timber culture, primarily through capital gains treatment of sales revenue coupled with current expensing of property taxes and interest outlays against ordinary income. This results, of course, in overallocation of the nation's limited capital stock to timber culture.

While interest and property taxes are expensable, planting costs, mainly labor, have to be capitalized. There is a bias to grow timber with a maximum input of time and a minimum input of labor. That is, if you spend money to restock cutover land right away, you cannot deduct the outlay for many years, so the present value of the deduction is negligible. But if you buy more land, and wait for nature to restock it untouched by human hand, you can deduct interest and taxes as current, ordinary expenses. Thus the tax man tells you to substitute land for labor, as well as for seedlings and other inputs of regeneration.

Vertically integrated firms have an incentive to shift profits from the mills to the woods in order to maximize the amount of income receiving capital gains treatment. The incentive is to let more value be added on the stump and less by processing in the mill. This again misallocates resources and, in addition, makes the timber business more capital intensive on the whole, and gives an invidious advantage to vertically integrated firms.

The Property Tax on Standing Timber

This tax is levied annually on a crop which ripens only periodically. It has been alleged that if immature timber were actually assessed on the *ad valorem* basis, no one could make a profit by restocking cutover land. Even if some might afford the long cash drain, it drives less wealthy people out of forestry since the tax must be paid over decades before stumpage is ripe for harvest.

Property tax liability actuates premature cutting. A forest owner subject to property taxation could never afford to hold timber long enough to realize the culmination of mean annual increment.

Since property taxation is local, the rates vary among taxing jurisdictions, forcing non-uniformity of forest management practices. Cruising timber for assessment purposes is costly relative to the tax revenues raised, and is likely to be inaccurate. Intensive forest management is discouraged, especially in the early stages of the growth cycle. (Capital invested early is taxed many times en route to harvest.) Full stocking is penalized by heavier taxes; and early stocking is penalized. The tax tells the owner to treat capital as an extra expensive input: to substitute land and labor for capital.

The tax is unrelated to benefits received from local government. Trees do not go to school, and forestry is capital intensive. Logging makes heavy use of migratory workers whose children are not schooled in the jurisdiction where the tax base is located, and for whom, some owners believe, they should not be responsible.

Arguments Pro the Property Tax on Standing Timber

Persuasive as those arguments may be, they do not entirely close the case. There are, surprisingly, points to make in favor of standing timber as a base for property taxation.

This tax is defensible in terms of uniformity; if capital in other forms (such as timber converted to lumber in houses) is subject to property taxation, then not to tax trees would be a subsidy. This is socially unwise because capital is scarce, and has many highly productive other uses. As to jobs, capital in timber has a lower employment multiplier than capital in most other forms. Capital combines with and employs labor basically when it turns over, and capital in standing timber turns over about as slowly as any capital you can think of. Likewise, the land under it employs labor mainly at harvest.

As an object lesson, consider public agencies holding timber exempt from property taxes. They have responded to this freedom from economic pressure by institutionalizing obsolescence in their doctrines and dogmas. Their thinking is sawlog bound, insisting on long rotations, and concepts of quality based on demand patterns of the past. They have ignored the marketing end of the business, the rapid advance of pulping and chipping technology with its new premium on shorter rotations. They have forgotten that growing timber is a means to consumer satisfaction and let it become an end in itself.

There is a long historical record of landowner behavior under property taxation, and it is not as catastrophic as its critics forecast. Small private owners subject to material property taxation have paid these taxes by practicing leaner, more economical forest management. The property tax on a pay-as-you-go basis gives the owner full equity in standing timber. This is in contrast with yield taxes, which are deferred to harvest and which let the government build up an equity in standing timber. From the public view, the property tax also therefore supplies a more steady and reliable revenue.

The cash flow problem of paying timber property taxes at the front end of a long investment cycle is not (as Mark Twain said of Wagner's music) really as bad as it sounds. In the early years the tax base is extremely low because of the low investment value of immature timber. (This refutes the allegation that the property tax treats buildings better than it does trees. The property tax on buildings is front-end loaded, and frequently produces serious, even fatal, cash flow crises at the beginning of life.) The impact of early property taxes is further reduced by their being expensable for income tax purposes, even though the income they generate is not to be taxed until harvest time.

The property tax bears relatively heavier on low site land than high site land* because of the naturally shorter optimal cycles on high site land. Besides, the naturally low values of many marginal sites will be totally wiped out by any substantial tax, thus precluding any forestry. While this is a complex topic, there is a case for retiring much marginal land, because the hidden public costs and subsidies of using it are very high, due to long hauls, steep slopes, and fragile environments.

---

* The author explains: "These are timberfolks' terms, counterintuitive to outsiders. 'High-site' means high-RENT site, where costs are low and values of the product (aka 'stumpage') high. It is likely to be warm, wet, flat, low, and near markets. 'Low-site' means low-RENT site: steep, remote, cold, dry, and remote from markets."

The Best Choice: Property Tax on Land

Many forest economists have touted a property tax based on the capacity of forest sites, exempting standing timber. This is analogous to the argument for using site value as the exclusive tax base in urban and other land uses. Where site productivity is the exclusive tax base there is no tax penalty on full stocking, nor yet on early stocking. On the contrary, the tax falling on bare land right after harvest exerts a great leverage to restock cutover land immediately. Here is a unique tax: it promotes land improvement, rather than suppressing it.

This tax base applies more pressure to the better sites; and no pressure to marginal ones, because there is no site productivity to serve as the tax base. We are talking about a pressure for stocking, not against use. Marginal sites often should remain unused. Thus the tax would act to curb "forestry sprawl," to keep down the costs of roading, hauling and runoff.

William Hyde, at Resources for the Future, and Ledyard and Moses at Northwestern, have given us profound analyses of the importance of encouraging intensive forest management on better sites and discouraging the overuse of remote marginal sites. The Federal Forest Service, exempt from any land tax pressure to economize on high sites, supplies the horrible object lesson. District Rangers are one big family. Why should good old Jake get less action, just because his district covers the high Rockies? So there is a little bit of everything, everywhere; no concentration of money and management on better land; and constant pressure to log fragile land at high cost in money, amenities and erosion.

The site value tax applies no pressure to prematurely cut. As timber stands approach maturity the value of standing timber becomes much higher than site value, so that land tax pressure is negligible. The pressure is all at the front end when there is nothing there but site value, and the pressure causes rapid restocking. (Like the tax on trees, the land tax is deductible for income tax purposes, moderating its effects.)

There is no inherent bias against capital intensive land use. There is a psychological pressure generated against long rotations because the opportunity cost of land is made explicit, but this is not a bias so much as it is clarification of market signals. (There will still be a market for wood products that demand long growth cycles.)

Like the tax on trees, this tax is pay-as-you-go with no buildup of government equity in mature timber. The revenues generated for local government are steady as a rock under this tax. They are independent of both harvest timing and stocking levels.

Pressure from Non-forest Uses

A vexing problem of forest taxation is the proper treatment of lands whose highest and best use is evolving into something other than commercial forestry: recreation, homesites, pasture, etc. *Ad valorem* land valuations give the owner of cutover land advance warning against restocking for commercial timber purposes, where the value is too high for forest use. Land assessments based on unconventional land uses have been regarded by foresters as an enemy, and in some sylvan counties no doubt they are, viewed in the small.

But consider the interlocking system of land use over the whole region. Market value assessments on land best suited for recreation hasten its conversion, thus meeting the demand and relieving pressure elsewhere. Other than outlawing recreation, this seems the only feasible way to contain "resort sprawl," and all the conflicts between amenities and logging. Let the market work; don't make a cult of obsolescence.

Sometimes mature timber becomes part of the recreational resource. Site productivity taxes with exemption of standing trees remove the major fiscal pressure to cut mature timber, leaving owners the option of holding it to integrate with the recreational enterprise if that is their judgment of what the market wants. This greatly increases their bidding power compared to timber culture, and defeats the aim of those who would protect commercial forests from resort users. (Yield taxes also remove pressure to cut, but look what else they do: they totally exempt the recreation owner who never cuts.)

Only the site tax is unbiased between competing land uses. If the site productivity concept is carried a step further, it removes from the tax base recreational buildings as well as all the capital used in the forest: private forest roads, log decks, camps, portable mills, fences, and all kinds of miscellaneous capital which is very hard to assess and is now treated nonuniformly.

If the policy is carried one step further yet, and made general for all land uses, it would mean the exemption from property tax of the best customers of the forest products industry. Forest interests have generally lined up against proposals to exempt urban buildings from property taxation. But I wonder if they have thought this one through. The sellers of saw logs would seem to be the greatest beneficiaries from the building boom that would ensue. Presumably they have been moved by the jeopardy that lower county taxes on urban buildings might imply higher tax demands on forests. But even if that be so, I would rather enjoy strong demand than low taxes, as a rule, if I have to choose.

Points Con the Site Value Tax for Forests

A much higher tax rate would be required to raise the same revenue as the present property tax which includes standing timber. Because of the higher rates, the accuracy of assessed values becomes more critical and a higher standard of assessment professionalism would be necessary. But this is not a bad thing, in my opinion. I agree with William the Conqueror, and many other noted state-builders, that a well-researched cadaster is central to the success of the kingdom.

If this tax policy is not general, that is if standing timber is exempt but capital in other forms in other industries is still taxed, it would draw marginal land into forestry. To offset this we would have to raise the rate on a special class of land identified as "forest land." The classification of land would necessarily be bureaucratized and, therefore, somewhat arbitrary at the fringes, and irritating to those who do not secure the classification they believe they deserve. It would also pose a large problem of continual reclassification at the margins as the nature of demand for forest land constantly evolves. Judging from the past, reclassification would always lag a generation behind the facts.

In the absence of classification and preferential treatment, this policy would subject forest land to valuations based on recreation, pasture or residential use. Some jurisdictions have addressed this problem by legislating that forest land assessments be based only on capitalized income from commercial forestry, screening out other influences on value.

The Bottom Line

If I am denied my first choice, then I would choose an income tax with restocking costs fully expensable, but property costs (interest and taxes) capitalized. This is the reverse of current practice. It would get cutover land restocked right away.

But the best base on all counts is site productivity, and I would generalize that case as far beyond forestry as possible.

The Alaska Permanent Fund: A Model of Resource Rents for Public Investment and Citizen Dividends

by Alanna Hartzok

I f you were a third grade student in the state of Alaska, one day in school you would play a game called Jennifer's Dilemma. The game tells the story of a little girl who has discovered a box of valuable coins. She must decide what to do with an unexpectedly large amount of money. It is a way for young children to learn about their own yearly windfall from the Alaska Permanent Fund. Since 2000, each Alaskan received an annual check averaging $1,386.

The Alaska Permanent Fund is a case study in a new concept of the role of government: that of agent to equitably distribute resource rents to the people, thereby securing common heritage rights to land and natural resources.

Purchased from Russia in 1867, Alaska became the 49th state in 1959. Under the Alaska Constitution* all the natural resources of Alaska belong to the state — to be used, developed and conserved for the maximum benefit of the people. Ten years after statehood, the first Prudhoe Bay oil lease sale yielded $900 million from oil companies for the right to drill oil on 164 tracts of state-owned land. That was a lot of money: in 1968, Alaska's total state budget was $112 million.

---

* Article VIII. Section 2: "General Authority: The legislature shall provide for the utilization, development, and conservation of all natural resources belonging to the State, including land and waters, for the maximum benefit of its people."

Rent as Public Revenue

Alaska's legislature decided to spend the original $900 million on basic community needs such as water and sewer systems, schools, airports, health and other social services.

Although their oil fields were very large, Alaskans came to agree that a portion of this wealth should be saved for the future when the oil runs out. In 1976 voters approved a constitutional amendment, proposed by Governor Jay Hammond and modified by the legislature, which placed in a permanent fund at least 25% of all mineral lease rentals, royalties, royalty sale proceeds, federal mineral revenue-sharing payments, and bonuses received by the State.

The Alaska Permanent Fund was thus established as a state institution with the task of responsibly administering and conserving oil and other resource royalties for the citizenry. Because the Fund was established as an inviolate trust, it serves to transform non-renewable oil wealth into a renewable source of wealth for future generations of Alaskans. The Fund's principal cannot be spent without a vote of the people. Decisions as to the use of the Fund's income are made each year by the legislature and the Governor.

Oil started flowing through the Trans-Alaska Pipeline in 1977, which was, at the time, the world's largest privately-financed construction project. In February of that year, the Fund received its first deposit of dedicated oil revenue of $734,000. For the next two decades, Alaskans debated what to do with those earnings to provide the best benefit for the most Alaskan citizens.

Like Jennifer with her box of coins, the dilemma was what to do with the growing income from the Fund. Would it best be saved for the future or managed as a development bank for Alaska's economy? After a four-year debate, the State Legislature decided to set up a trust. The Alaska Permanent Fund Corporation was created to manage the assets of the Fund.

The same year the Legislature also created the Permanent Fund Dividend Program, retroactive to January 1, 1979, to distribute a portion of the income of the Permanent Fund each year to eligible Alaskans as a dividend payment. By the end of 1982, after a couple years of wrangling with the US Supreme Court over constitutional details,* all residents of Alaska — every woman, man and child who

---

* The court ruled, in Zobel v. Williams (1982) that differential payments based on years of residence were an unconstitutional burden on interstate travel.

could show they had lived in Alaska for at least a year received their first $1,000 dividend. Thus began Alaska's annual program of paying each of its citizens a share of the wealth from publicly owned resources.

In 1987 the Permanent Fund Dividend Division was created within the Department of Revenue to consolidate responsibilities for the administration and operation of the dividend program. Through this program, the Fund puts more new money into the state's economy than the total payroll of any industry in Alaska except the US military, petroleum and the civilian federal government. Compared to the wages paid to Alaskans by basic industry, dividends make a greater contribution than the seafood industry, construction, tourism, timber, mining and agriculture. For a considerable percentage of Alaskans, the dividend adds more than ten percent to the income of their family. This is particularly true in rural Alaska.

There is strong citizen interest in the Fund's operation and investment activities. Earnings of the Fund undergo special public scrutiny since any expenditure of such earnings must be subject to the legislative appropriation process. Colorful, detailed publications, including an Annual Report, describe the various components of the Fund. Under the policy guidance of the Fund's six trustees and the corporation's executive director and staff, there has developed an extensive accountability program and open meetings with opportunity for citizen participation.

The Alaska Permanent Fund Corporation website[†] keeps current all investment and distribution activities of the Fund. The history of the development of the Fund, its incorporation, details concerning its management, along with up-to-date information on the Fund portfolio and dividend pay-out amounts. The Permanent Fund's website also offers lesson plans (such as "Jennifer's Dilemma") and other teaching materials. Public inquiries at the site receive prompt, knowledgeable replies.

The Alaska Permanent Fund is a well-managed, transparent and democratic institution. It is a pioneering model of a fair, effective way to secure common heritage wealth benefits for the people of a state. While undoubtedly an institution worthy of

† www.apfc.org

replication worldwide, there are, however, aspects of the Fund which upon close examination reveal a dilemma.

Charlie's Challenge and the Prudent Investor Rule

Let's imagine now that Jennifer has given Uncle Charlie some of her valuable coins to invest in the best, safest way possible. Jennifer trusts Uncle Charlie to do a good job because he is an expert investor. Charlie invests in a diversified portfolio of stocks, bonds and other securities, including real estate. Having carefully explored potential investments in "the lower 48", Charlie selects several properties, including one in the City of Philadelphia. Philadelphia has low property taxes, state and federal monies pouring into the city and "free enterprise zones" — so real estate in this city looks like a good investment for Jennifer.

Then, however, Charlie learns that a growing citizens movement in Philadelphia is set on capturing, for its people, the rent of another highly valuable natural resource — the city's land sites. Charlie understands that Philadelphians are simply trying to establish the same sort of program that has been such a benefit to Alaskans. Yet if the movement for land value taxation in Philadelphia succeeds, it will cut into the profits for Jennifer's investment fund! How will Charlie respond? Will he try to thwart the LVT movement in Philly, even though he recognizes its justice? Or will he forego real estate investments, to the detriment of Jennifer's income?

In fact, there was a growing citizens movement for land value taxation in Philadelphia, that was gaining headway around 2000. Its momentum was beaten back by a well-financed campaign waged by a small group of powerful real estate interests, though it still survives in Philadelphia and other cities. Even if there is little immediate threat to Jennifer's real estate investments, Charlie still faces an ethical challenge. Knowing the basic justice of Alaska's program to redistribute resource-rent income to its citizens, is it right for him to contribute to other citizens, in other states, being denied theirs?

In 2017 the Fund's endowment stands at $59.9 billion. It is now large enough that it has the power to grab significant amounts of resource rents from many different places. Within established foundation guidelines of the "prudent investor rule," the Trustees' goal is to earn better-than-average rates of return with below-average levels of risk. Under normal investment rules, there are no compelling ethical criteria for investing. In fact, the Fund makes a special point that one way in which it minimizes risk is that it avoids "social" or "political" investing.

In other words, mandated by law to secure the continued prosperity of the citizens of Alaska now and into the future, the Fund is in the position to make substantial profits from land and natural resources all over the world, via Fund investments in real estate and stocks. As a smart, ethical Alaskan, Charlie understands the importance of securing the value of natural resources for the people's benefit. He can see that Alaska's efficient permanent fund is now contributing to the stealing of others' resource rents, through "normal, legal and prudent" investment mechanisms.

As people all over the world begin to awaken to and indeed demand their rights to the rents of common heritage resources, investment portfolios will have to change. Sooner or later, the Alaska Permanent Fund, along with other investment funds, will have to look elsewhere to generate profits — perhaps to investments in renewable energy technologies which could help everyone when the oil runs dry.

Resource Rights and Territorial Claims

The state of Alaska receives federal money for several substantial military installations. The military is established to protect the territory of the United States and this protection secures the rights to US land and resources for the people of the US (as well as foreigners who have legal title to American lands). The military, paid for by US citizens out of federal income taxes, is protecting Alaskan citizens' rights to the resource royalties they are now collecting through the Fund. Thus, all US citizens contribute to the value of Alaska's oil resources and thus to the dividends paid to Alaskans — but they get no value in return.

The Fund is also a source of loans to the US government via US savings bonds. Taxpayers from the other 49 states pay interest on the federal debt — a portion of which is owned by the Fund! And where, one might ask, are the Alaska Permanent Fund equivalents for the other oil producing and mineral mining states?* Many corporation owners of oil and mineral lands pay no federal taxes at all. They engage in other ventures such as agribusiness at a loss, write the loss off against their oil profits, and end up with no taxable income on the books.

The unique situation of the Alaska Permanent Fund — a sovereign fund, asserting the rights of a state's citizens to the value of its natural resources in perpetuity, yet maintaining and increasing its endowment by investing in rights to natural resources in other sovereign states and nations — brings up questions of territorial rights in ways that are seldom considered. Let's check in again with Jennifer and Uncle Charlie. What would Jennifer do if someone informed her that the box of coins was theirs, that they had found it first, and now they wanted it back?

If Jennifer refuses to surrender her coins to the prior claimant, conflict would likely arise. Uncle Charlie might supply Jennifer with some really big guns or funds for an extensive court battle. Territory was always there; like Jennifer's coins, it had a prior claimant, and therefore "territorial rights" are always established by force: either explicitly in the sense of armed conflict, or implicitly by means of enforceable agreements.

Upon what basis is the exclusive claim of the people of Alaska to the oil resources of Alaska? Let us consider the history of this claim.

The state takes its name from the Eskimo word "Alakshak." The "prior claim" by original occupancy would appear to be that of the indigenous people.

Russia claimed Alaska by right of discovery[†] after it was sighted by Vitus Bering in 1741. Purchase was negotiated by

---

* Not to mention the immense values of many other natural resources, such as rivers, lakes and timber lands — and, especially, the most valuable natural resource of them all: urban land sites.

† The legal doctrine of discovery, famously articulated by Chief Justice John Marshall in Johnson v. M'Intosh (1823), provided a rationale for the claiming of aboriginal land by colonial settlers, whose governments recognized common-law systems of private land ownership that aboriginal societies lacked. Thus, the European colonial power "established" a land-tenure system where, in terms of its legal system, none had existed before.

the US government's Secretary of State William H. Seward who bought Alaska from Russia in 1867 for $7.2 million, about two cents an acre. The purchase by, and transfer of rights to, the United States was considered legitimate on the basis of Russia's prior claim by discovery.

During World War II the United States sent thousands of workers to Alaska to build defense installments and the Alaska Highway. In 1942 the Japanese occupied several Aleutian islands, the only part of North America that was invaded during the war, and US troops fought to remove them. Thus the US government demonstrated its willingness to defend Alaska as part of its sovereign territory.

Alaska's constitution establishes its people's right to the oil resources of Alaska. This should be recognized as an important human rights achievement. The very fact that the Alaska Permanent Fund profits from investment in natural resources in other states shows how (unfortunately) unconventional this arrangement is. Nevertheless, Alaska's sovereign control over its resources for the benefit of its people may not be inviolate.

Suppose Jennifer's family is not well-to-do, and her trove of coins had been left there by a family member, to help the whole family through hard times. In that case, should Jennifer be permitted to spend them just as she wants? If a territory contains resources that contribute to the well-being of everyone else on earth, then it can be argued that absolute control of those resources by the people of that territory would give them undue power and control over the people of the rest of the world.

The basis upon which the citizens of Alaska stake their exclusive claim to the oil and natural resources of Alaska is a complex historical weaving of territorial claims by discovery, purchase, military might and democratic law. Yet it is not clear whether these components add up to a sufficient ethical basis for an exclusive claim. People around the world pay Alaska to extract its oil. Furthermore, Alaska's oil revenues, for the exclusive benefit of Alaska's people, are invested in assets whose value derives, in large part, from the natural resources of other states and nations.

Alaska's constitution simply establishes the Fund as a legal entity without stating any moral or ethical claims. However, it is widely believed that there is a moral hierarchy to territorial claims — that some are more right than others. Ultimately, the only moral and ethical basis upon which the citizens of Alaska can assert a claim to Alaska's oil resources is by birthright to the gifts of nature. And that cannot be an exclusive claim, because the citizens of Alaska cannot claim a greater right to those resources than any other people. As we have seen, exclusive claims to natural resources are made on the basis of force and convention. If all human beings have equal rights, including to the world's natural opportunities, then there can be no moral justification for exclusive ownership of those resources, either by individuals or by groups.

The Alaska Permanent Fund, as a prudently managed investment trust, cannot avoid these ethical contradictions.

How could the Alaska Permanent Fund set itself on surer moral ground? It could seek a broader, global, humanitarian role for the Fund — for example, it could assist people in other parts of the world to secure their own fair-share rights to resource rents.

For instance, Africa now accounts for some ten percent of US oil imports (it had been more until recently). Many African countries with oil wealth do not publish their oil revenue in the national budgets. These nations are rife with strife, civil war, corruption and poverty. Humanitarian organizations and many African citizens are calling for transparency and accountability in the management of oil funds and for the use of oil wealth for overall economic development. The Alaska Permanent Fund could play an important role by sharing its expertise with these nations to help them establish similar funds.

Additionally, the Fund could develop a screen for its investments. It could decide *not* to invest in land and resource securities and instead *to* invest primarily in the development of renewable energy technology, and in places and in ways that would support the emergence of governing principles aligned with the primary task of the Fund: the collection of resource rents as a common heritage right for all people.

It would be a big step in the right direction if people all over the world awakened to their claim to the resources of their state, or nation, as the Alaskans did. But this would be insufficient to secure justice in land rights, because some nation states are large and well-endowed with land and resources, while others are small or lack natural resources.

Global Resource Agency

These imbalances could be remedied by the creation of a Global Resource Agency which would function in some ways similar to, but much more extensively than, the Alaska Fund. The Global Resource Agency could be responsible for (1) monitoring the global commons (the atmosphere and oceans); (2) determining rules for access to transnational resources (such as forests, rivers and lakes, electromagnetic spectrum and satellite orbital zones); (3) issuing use permits; and (4) collecting resource royalties and revenues.

Fees collected from common heritage resources worldwide could be equitably distributed, according to formulas based on population and development criteria. For example, a percentage of the oil rents from the Alaska Permanent Fund could be collected by the Global Resource Agency and either distributed directly to citizens in regions with no oil resources in a kind of dividend sharing program, or made available as interest free loan funds for sustainable development projects in those areas.

The Global Resource Agency could fund institutions and activities needed for global environmental protection, justice, and peacekeeping, such as the World Court and the International Criminal Court. This would in turn contribute to a better and more secure quality of life for the citizens of Alaska and elsewhere who would pay a portion of their resource rents into the GRA. The principle that the earth is the birthright of all on an equal basis would also guide legal decisions made by the courts in determining just solutions to territorial disputes.

Such an institution would take years to establish and to become accepted. While some nation states, strongly controlled by vested interests in the current system, would balk at the idea of a Global Resource Agency, others would see its potential to promote stability and economic fair play for their people. The Alaska Permanent Fund could provide visionary leadership in this process.

Some people might object to the idea of a Global Resource Agency out of fears that it would add another top-heavy level of bureaucracy to an already governmentally burdened world. But those advocating strengthened global governance ask us to imagine the shape of the emerging world as a pyramid with three basic levels: a small tier at the top for global institutions, a greatly slimmed down second band of national governments, and a vast sturdy base of local government. The key insight is that in this model, the primary role of governance on each tier to collect and redistribute land and resource rents for the benefit of all. Most of the revenues raised, decisions made and benefits provided would be at the local level.

The Game has Changed

The object of the 4000 year old Chinese game of Go is to gain control of territory by capturing enemy stones on a board. You win by forming walls with your stones that surround more territory than do your opponent's walls. Go is based on the concept that if you possess land or territory, you have liberty and freedom. Without land or territory, you have nothing to base life on; you are without life: dead.

Chess, probably invented in India in ancient times, was widespread in Europe in the 16th century when the rules were finalized. More directly confrontational than GO, chess exhibits the same theme of territorial conquest and control as a life or death affair.

When the world was too big for any one army to conquer, capturing and holding territory made sense as a kind of organizing principle. Now, we live in world in which global annihilation, either through war or ecocide, is a real possibility. "Winning" by taking away the territory of the "other" now has a boomerang effect, as numerous intractable civil wars attest. Time, attention, energy and money devoted to securing or maintaining exclusive claim to particular territory now needs to be redirected to serve the needs of the entire community and, indeed, the planet.

As we keep these sobering facts in mind, it is worth noting that the Alaska Permanent Fund, based on the democratic constitutional equal right to natural resources, though not a perfect model, is nonetheless one of the most enlightened governmental "works in progress" in our world today.

Tax Treatment of Land Income

by Mason Gaffney

R emember when market economics "triumphed" over socialism? Since then, it has exhibited more than enough failures to temper our hubris. Among them: growing concentration of economic power, stagnant or falling real wage rates, homelessness and beggary, chronic unemployment, growing crime rates and personal insecurity, obsolescence in the face of rising foreign competition, dangerous dependence on oil, growing recourse to the underground economy, falling literacy and educational attainments, anomie and substance addiction, rampant self-seeking and predation and rising social divisions leading toward class warfare.

The structural flaw in capitalism is our tolerance of unearned income and wealth. The idea of free markets is that income should go to incite and reward productive activity; wealth should incite and reward saving and capital formation. Unearned income and wealth do neither. Unearned wealth today (like slave-owning in the past) actually deters saving by the fairly obvious route of satisfying the owners' need for the security of wealth, without their actually creating any capital.

The tragedy for capitalism is that the role of unearned wealth is kept invisible. That was one of the goals of J. B. Clark and other pioneers of "neo-classical" economics. For a century, scholars have succeeded in distorting the concepts and data needed to lay bare the problem. In the face of vested interest and blinkered scholarship, statesmen miss the main point and formulate wrong policies.

Many conservatives argue for decreasing the tax on capital

gains, in order to encourage "venture capital" and raise the rate of return-after-taxes on new investments. In 1987, when President Bush (Sr.) was proposing such a cut, Professor James Poterba estimated that "venture capital" accounted for only about 1% of capital gains. That encourages a suspicion much of "capital" gains come from old assets — particularly land.

Most modern Georgists believe the property tax is the best means to tap rent, but it is not the only means. Income taxes socialize billions in land rent — and could socialize much more. The first task for Georgist reformers is to seal off landowners' escape route from property taxation. Landowners' strategy has long been to secure property tax relief by raising income taxes, while converting the income tax into mainly a payroll tax.

An allied issue is how to spur domestic capital formation. It's claimed that this will be stimulated by lowering capital gains taxes. What issue could be more Georgist than capital formation? "Tax land to untax capital" is the Georgist idea. The aim of untaxing capital is to free up forces that induce investment and create new capital.

To do that we need policies that distinguish old capital from new — a key difference that is recognized by many economists. More basically, we need recognize that "old capital," as commonly defined, includes the oldest asset of all: land. We must distinguish man-made capital, the fruit of saving and real investment, from natural resources or land. It is the *old* capital, and mainly land, that yield "capital" gains.

The beauty and vigor and challenge of Georgist reform is precisely its immediate relevance to a wide range of public issues. Some challenge it in terms of its attainability. It may call for changes in some public attitudes, working uphill against wealthy and antisocial powers, but it is attainable in the sense that it calls for no more than minor tweaks in existing institutions. Anti-Georgists would love to narrow Georgism to the one modest goal of reforming local real estate taxation. I honor and support those who focus on the attainable goal of urban property tax transformation, and hope I may be counted among them. Let's redouble those efforts, but let us also move into the larger public dialogue on the grand issues George used to inspire and move a generation.

So long as we have income taxes, it is a Georgist policy to

see that land pays more income tax, and earned income pays less. The income tax taps a lot of land rent, and also commands the public dialogue. Henry George himself called income taxation a second choice — not first, but not last either. George and Georgists were "present at the creation" of the American income tax. You will be surprised at what a key role they played. Let's review some history.

Congress enacted an income tax in 1894. There were fifty Populists in the House then, and six avowed Georgists. They all supported an amendment to the income tax act, by Judge James Maguire of California, to make it a direct tax on land rents. The amendment failed, but we still owe a debt to those six.* We may reasonably surmise a bloc of six committed, zealous Congressmen, several within a larger bloc of fifty Populists, was what kept land rents in the base of the 1894 Act, blocking any income tax bill that excluded land income. This in turn provoked the Supreme Court into holding the 1894 Act unconstitutional, on grounds that a "direct" tax had to be apportioned among states by population. (Such apportionment was unacceptable in Congress, just as James Madison and Alexander Hamilton had planned a century earlier.) Since they couldn't get an income tax exempting rents, income taxers were forced into engineering the 16th Amendment (1913) which removed the original constitutional roadblock to direct taxation of land rents. Congress has been taxing land rents ever since. It never had before.

It even has the power, if it wishes, to exempt all other forms of income and limit the tax to rent. Is that an impossible dream? Not really. The maligned corporation income tax is a tax purely on property income. In the 1960s new capital achieved partial *de facto* exemption via fast write-off. Expensing is tantamount to total exemption. If we tax the profits of property, and relieve new capital, what is being taxed but land rent? We had a "graded tax plan" nationally, and never knew it!

Eight decades of creeping regress

Reviving the capital gains exclusion would nearly complete an anti-Georgist transformation of the income tax to a tax on the

---

* Tom Johnson and Michael Harter of Ohio; Jerry Simpson, Kansas; John de Witt Warner and Charles Tracy, New York; James Maguire, California

work and enterprise of the median citizen. Here is a list of the anti-Georgist changes to date. They are enough to make a Georgist feel like a chess player facing mate.

a. Wage and salary withholding came in 1941, along with higher rates in lower brackets, converting a tax primarily on property income into a mass payroll tax. State and local public employees, previously exempt, were added to the base in 1939.
b. "Bracket creep" during inflation pushed workers into higher rate brackets, with no increase of real income. This effect has been reinforced at the bottom, where most wage and salary income is found.
c. At the top, where most rents and capital gains are, the top rate was lowered from 70% to 28%.
d. Corporations, meanwhile, are immune to bracket creep because the corporate rate is basically flat (with trivial exceptions at the bottom). The corporate share of total tax revenues has fallen sharply. In addition, In 1986 Congress lowered the flat corporate rate from 46% to 34%.
e. Preferential treatment of land rents and gains has grown in several dimensions, as we will discuss.

The cumulative effect of those changes has been to utterly transform the income tax. A tax on the privileges of the idle rich ("idle" meaning those who enjoy unearned income) has become a tax on the necessities and earnings of the working poor.

The shift of taxes off rent-yielding property is the more striking when we add in the States. In 1920 fully 50% of State revenues came from State property taxes; today hardly any does. Nearly all local revenues were then from property; today much less than half is. Sales and income taxes (at various levels) have replaced them.

One bright, or at least light gray spot in this dark history was the relief of new investment from taxation under JFK, in a compact known as "business Keynesianism." CEA chair Walter Heller sold the idea of offsetting the effect of high income tax rates by allowing fast write-off of most new investments, plus an investment tax credit (ITC). The high tax rate applies in full force to land rents; new investment gets major relief. Net result: an income tax that achieves nationally the same goal property tax reformers have to chip at laboriously from town to town. It was not a golden age, but neither was it an age of rust. It was a time when the economy refused to take its expected dive. Investors who responded to the lures of accelerated depreciation, and lawyers who worked on intricate moves to exploit them, never dreamed they were responding to ideas originating with a radical reformer from the 19th century.

The provenance of Heller's idea shows the influence of a Georgist academic, John R. Commons (1862-1945), a leading "Institutionalist" thinker at The University of Wisconsin. Commons's views on taxing land and exempting capital and wages are set forth strongly in his *Institutional Economics:*

> *"... the man who gets his wealth by mere rise in site-values should pay proportionately higher taxes than the one who gets his wealth by industry or agriculture. In the one case he extracts wealth from the commonwealth without adding to it. In the other case he contributes directly to an increase in both private wealth and commonwealth."*

Commons favored the fast write-off of new investments, the very idea Walter Heller put across in Washington. His purpose was explicitly to make the income tax bear heavier on land rents than on the returns to capital. When the purpose of Congress is really to encourage new investment, fast write-off of new capital is the obvious tool.

In 1986 Congress eliminated the preferential treatment of new investment in real capital formation. The three changes were: 1) Repeal of Investment Tax Credit (ITC); 2) Lengthening tax lives; 3) Decelerating depreciation pathways. Thus, the effective tax rate on most new investment was raised. Traditional liberals applauded this as closing loopholes; economists, conservative or liberal, have been enchanted by "uniformity." Uniformity between mutually convertible things is a good rule — but land and capital are *in*convertible, so incentive taxation may treat them differently.

Before 1986 a high-bracket professional — physician, lawyer or actor — could avoid the effects of high marginal tax rates by investing in certain kinds of real new capital: buildings, equipment, machines, rolling stock, furnishings and fixtures, trees or livestock. This did, it is true, make for overcapacity in certain kinds of capital, e.g. avocado trees in California, or offices in Texas. Some forms of capital received much more exemption than others; I do not defend the abuse. But today that professional is better off buying up old capital and land. Corporations, meanwhile, join the merger-mania which creates no new wealth at all.

The main effect of untaxing land gains is simply to redistribute wealth and overprice land. Incentives to buy and hold land will raise the demand, not the supply. Such incentives stimulate the production of nothing and the employment of no one. They simply raise asking price and exclude marginal buyers from the market.

Covert depreciation of land

In the tax code, land is not depreciable, and should not enjoy the benefits of any write-off. This is obviously part of the heritage we owe to Judge James Maguire, Warren Worth Bailey and others present at the creation. Left to their own devices, standard-brand economists like John Bates Clark and Frank Knight would have made land depreciable, for they maintained vehemently that land is no different from other capital.

But the Internal Revenue Code still says land is different. When an investor buys land under an old grove, or old building, the Code says he must allocate his basis between the depreciable capital and the non-depreciable land. The requirement is reasonable, since buildings and fruit trees generally lose value with time, while land does not. So far, so good — but, as the watchdogs dozed, IRS became extremely lax and "generous" in letting buyers overallocate basis to the depreciable building or grove of trees. Thus they contrive to depreciate for income tax not just the building or trees, but a major part of the land value.

The IRS invites taxpayers to use the local property tax assessor's allocation between land and buildings. Here is another intimate relationship of income and property taxation. Underassessing land for property taxation actually has more impact on income taxes than on property taxes. The same property tax rate is applied to both land and buildings — but buildings are depreciable for income tax, and land is not. Reams of evidence have been published finding these assessors' allocations consistently understate land values relative to building values.

Most remarkably, land is written off again and again, every

time taxable property changes hands. Every succeeding owner overallocates his basis to depreciable capital, setting himself up to depreciate the land again. Thus every piece of land may be partly written off as many times as it sells. In result, the contribution of much land to tax revenues is negative, and heavily so.

Land appreciation produces nothing

Increased land values are not caused by holding title to and "financing" appreciating land; interest payments do not "produce" increments to land value. Appreciation would occur anyway.* An owner needn't be allowed to deduct his "carrying costs," his costs of holding title, in order to make land rise in value. Demand makes it rise, not cost.

The only functional reason for deducting carrying costs, then, is to avoid discriminating between equity holders and mortgaged holders of title. This encourages the pledging land as security for loans.† An owner has not created land but simply outbid everyone else for it. Supply is fixed. Non-deductibility would simply lower the price, possibly broadening entry into the market.

When a land developer pays out for streets and their improvements, these are deductible over some period. The capital in streets wears out, like all capital, but what the developer bought for his outlay is the community's duty to maintain, repair, police, service and replace those streets forever. That benefit is capitalized into land prices. The premium of urban value over farm value is thus acquired by spending deductible money. It's tantamount to writing off part of the cost of land purchase.

Aren't excessive depreciations eventually taxed?

Anyone defending the system would insist the Treasury recoups excess depreciation when property is sold. Thus the tax exemption is not perpetual, but is finally recognized and taxed at time of sale.

---

* While it is true that changes in interest rates affect land values, this is not something that the landholder does, except, perhaps, as part of a political class. — Ed.

† This is an inadvisable practice that leads to greater economic volatility; see Gaffney, *After the Crash: Designing a Depression-free Economy*

The basic preference for land gains is tax deferral. Land gains are not recognized and taxed as income when they accrue, but only later upon sale for cash. To grasp the advantage of this deferral, consider two investors, Alice and Bob. Both are subject to a tax rate of 50%.

Alice puts $1 in a savings account paying 7.2% compounded annually. (That is the rate at which money doubles every ten years.) She gets 3.6% after taxes, and plows it back, at which rate it takes twice as long, twenty years, for money to double. After sixty years her wealth has grown to $8.

Bob puts his $1 in land whose value rises at 7.2% per year. After sixty years its value has doubled 6 times, to $64. He sells it and pays taxes of 50% on the gain of $63. He thus clears $32.50 after taxes. Bob's wealth has grown to over 4 times Alice's wealth, although both made the same rate of return, and both paid taxes at the same rate. The difference is timing.

A long period of tax deferral, tantamount to tax exemption, is still very advantageous, considering the time value of money. Such laggard treatment is in stark contrast with the unforgiving withholding and full rates levied on salaries, wages and current profits from the "ordinary" functions of producing goods and services. It seems that paying taxes promptly "is what the simple folk do."

Furthermore, landowners routinely defeat recoupment. Excess depreciation, and unrecouped deduction of carrying costs, have accumulated over several generations, continue to accumulate, and will accumulate in perpetuity until the system is radically revised.

Recoupment is a certainty only for careless taxpayers, or pinched taxpayers who lack room to maneuver. In general, excess depreciation is not recouped. Tax exemption is achieved in perpetuity — and the next generation does it again! Landowners have been running circles around Georgists because Georgists have foolishly taken their eyes off the income tax, which raises more revenue than any other tax. While we had our noses to the grindstone of local policy, Congress gave away the store.

The income tax, the dream of Warren Worth Bailey, evolved into a nightmare. It became class legislation, the more sinister because invisible. Everyone in 18th century France knew the landed nobles were tax-exempt, but few modern Americans, economists or not, have much knowledge or insight into what very preferential tax treatment is accorded to land gains.

Much land has been written off already, some in part, some whole, and some more than 100%. In general it is a good rule to let bygones be bygones. In this case, however, the next tax reformer might with justice declare the state has already purchased the land, some of it more than once. "The state" as such may have no moral standing, but it has purchased the land with money extracted from income earned by useful working and investing.

Income taxation can be constructive and useful if we follow Commons's counsel to tax "personal (work effort) income at the lowest…; investment incomes at a medium…; site value incomes at the highest rates, also progressive on large holdings." Land gains should be fully taxed as they accrue, using any of various methods proposed by William Vickrey, James Wetzler or Mason Gaffney. Locked-in effects can be more than offset by coupling gains taxes with annual property taxes, as Taiwan does.

The result would be greatly to strengthen capitalism — meaning by this a system where capital proper — a.k.a. capital goods — is privately owned and free of punitive taxation. Now, all property and property income are tainted by association with unearned income from land. Removing this taint would help purify property in theory, ideology and practice.

Appendix:Rent-seeking outlays

Ownership of natural resources, *de facto* or *de jure*, is often given in return for occupying and/or using the resource first. "Grandfather rights" is a generic name for this. Rational rent-seekers incur deductible losses today, as an investment to secure the resource. These losses are basically costs of acquiring land, and should not be written off at all, yet they are. Current operating losses are expensible; capital outlays are at least depreciable.

Water law. Riparian rights are secured by the appropriative doctrine: "first in time, first in right." Prior use establishes a perpetual license. The only way to secure the future rents is develop and use the water now, before a rival. The winner absorbs the losses of premature use, and deducts them from taxable income — thus the fisc shares the cost of land acquisition.

Zoning. The race is to get grandfathered in on NIMBY or LULU (Locally Undesirable Land Use) activities before they are zoned out. The more offensive a land use is to its neighbors, the more lucrative for a firm to establish an early history of noise, traffic, on-street parking, odors, high-rise building, crowding lot lines, smoke, fumes and other nuisances.

Air pollution. The current approach is not to make the polluter pay, but to reward him with an "offset right," a pollution right he may keep and use, or sell to others if he abates his own. "His own" is based on his history of prior pollution, which thus acquires a positive market value. The incentive is to pollute liberally today to secure the offset right tomorrow. Losses incurred are deductible; offset rights, if sold, yield "capital gains." The pliability and corruption of the word "capital" is remarkable.

Radio spectrum. Rights are allocated the same way. The license is "free," but one must use it or lose it. The incentive is to use it prematurely, suffering losses, taking the gain in the rising value of the license as demand rises. Rights to air routes, and time-slots and gates at airports, were allocated the same way (although some of these were lost during deregulation).

Mineral rights. Exploration costs for oil, gas and hardrock minerals are largely expensible, but mineral deposits, once found, are "capital" assets for tax purposes. There is a long list of other tax favors for minerals, too long to recite here; it is discussed elsewhere.* Once one gets the concept, one sees more and more resources, or sticks in the bundle of rights to resources, being distributed on this appropriative principle. Familiar concepts and phrases are squatters' rights, use it or lose it, prior possession, homesteading, franchise, trade territory, adverse possession, history of use, customary rights, grandfather protection, established use, etc. All these are ways of acquiring landownership, *de jure* or *de facto*, by incurring early losses.

---

* See Mason Gaffney, "Oil and Gas: the Unfinished Tax Reform"

Global Resources

by Lindy Davies

A t this moment in history, a great many people have come to believe that society really must get serious about climate change. Skeptics complain about the conjectural nature of "the science" on this issue. However, a serious problem can exist, even if its effects cannot be predicted with certainty. No one knows for sure how severe the consequences of unchecked greenhouse-gas warming will be, or when things will start to get really bad. We will assume here that human activity is the main cause of the current wave of climate change, and that if greenhouse gas production continues unchecked, catastrophic change is probable.

For most people, in most communities, a credible risk of a dire outcome is enough to motivate action. The chance of a home burning to the ground is pretty low, yet homeowners routinely invest in fire insurance, smoke detectors and fire extinguishers. Communities build levees, not to protect against high tide, but against hundred-year flooding events.

Yet people don't always respond rationally to risks. The likelihood of a terrorist attack in the United States is very small. The collapse of a busy highway bridge is much more likely. The Federal Highway Administration estimated in 2013 that about one quarter of the 607,000 bridges in the United States are functionally obsolete. Nevertheless, the 9/11 attacks so traumatized Americans that they are willing to devote far greater resources to guarding against terrorists than to repairing bridges. The risks of climate change include flooding, sea level rise, extreme weather, drought, mass migrations and resource wars — yet society has been unwilling to commit more than token resources to curbing greenhouse-gas emissions. A feasible plan for dealing with this problem would have to include a strategy for dealing with this cognitive dissonance.

This issue is a natural one for Georgists, who have long proclaimed that "the Earth is the birthright of all [hu]mankind." Georgists believe that the value of land is the natural fund for public goods and services — and that "economic land" is properly understood to mean not just surface locations, but natural opportunities of all kinds. The economic category of land includes, for example, broadcast frequencies, subsurface mineral rights, locations in geosynchronous orbit — and the capacity of air and water to absorb and disperse waste materials. Our discussion of *global* resources centers on this last form of natural opportunity.

It seems appropriate to approach this discussion in terms of four key questions: 1) What resources are specifically global in character? 2) How are these resources to be quantified and assessed? 3) Under what jurisdictional authority should their value be collected and distributed? and 4) How can the entrenched resistance to this program be overcome, so that it can actually be implemented?

It's interesting to note that these issues were beyond the ken of the original COLT manual, though it was compiled in the late 1960s, a time of burgeoning ecological awareness, when Apollo VIII's portrait of Mother Earth was at its most iconic. The COLT manual's only discussion of global resources was a page on the emerging United Nations Convention on the Law of the Sea, which at that time was only under discussion, first emerging as an international agreement in 1973. That agreement did mention the need to preserve the ecological health of the oceans, but offered no enforceable mechanism for doing so. It was much more concerned with national concerns, such as the limits of fishing and mining rights in territorial waters, and of military installations. However, the agreement had one small, but telling, provision showing recognition of the seas as a communal resource: it gave landlocked states the right of free access to the sea.*

What are global resources?

A truly global resource is one that cannot be subjected to any national jurisdiction — because every person and nation has the

---

* See United Nations, "Convention on the Law of the Sea"

same relationship to it. This isn't as radical an idea as it may appear. We are accustomed to dealing with transboundary resources. For example, the Hudson River is a state resource; its entire length is within the boundaries of New York State. The Mississippi River, on the other hand, is a national resource; it flows through ten states. The Jordan River, which flows through some of the most contentious territory in the world, is an international resource. So is the Colorado River, which the United States usually sucks dry before its waters can reach its mouth in Mexico. Transboundary resources such as these, however, do not have a global character. Disputes over them can be negotiated by the affected sovereign states.

This cannot be said of the atmospheric and oceanic commons. A truly global resource cannot be localized and parceled out. This is not to say that every aspect of the air and the sea has this global character; some parts of them can indeed be localized. If, say, tire plants in Ohio pollute the air with sulfur dioxide, and prevailing weather patterns deposit this pollution, in the form of acid rain, in Vermont, then Vermont's sovereign air-space has been compromised by Ohio's polluters. The damage is localized, and Vermont's acid rain problem can be dealt with as a regional issue. Or, if a rich mineral deposit is discovered on the deep ocean floor, the right to mine that resource can be codified by treaty among sovereign nations. The mineral resource is not "global" simply because it had not yet been claimed. Many resources on dry land were initially unclaimed, free for the taking. When land claims began to be disputed, governments began to adopt rules governing them. Similarly, locations in high-Earth orbit have been discovered to have great value as sites for communications satellites. Such sites, previously just valueless dots in outer space, have since been localized, and rights to their use have been codified in treaties.[†]

When we talk about global climate change, we must realize that the resources in question, the atmosphere and the oceans, are not localizable — their location is the entire planet. The utility of the resources are their capacity to harmlessly absorb wastes which disperse into the entire system. This capacity once seemed limitless. We have recently come to understand, though, that there are limits: the air and sea will not soak up our combustion products forever

---

† See United Nations, "Space Law Treaties and Principles"

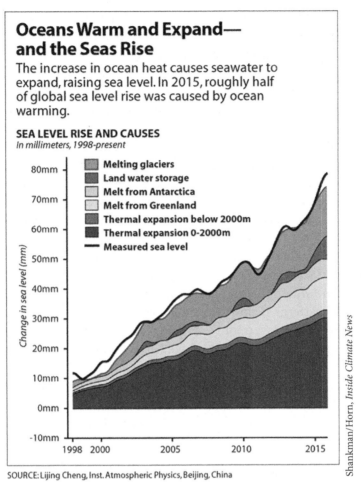

Oceans Warm and Expand—and the Seas Rise

The increase in ocean heat causes seawater to expand, raising sea level. In 2015, roughly half of global sea level rise was caused by ocean warming.

SEA LEVEL RISE AND CAUSES
In millimeters, 1998-present

Legend:
- Melting glaciers
- Land water storage
- Melt from Antarctica
- Melt from Greenland
- Thermal expansion below 2000m
- Thermal expansion 0-2000m
- Measured sea level

Change in sea level (mm) — y-axis: -10mm, 0mm, 10mm, 20mm, 30mm, 40mm, 50mm, 60mm, 70mm, 80mm

x-axis: 1998, 2000, 2005, 2010, 2015

SOURCE: Lijing Cheng, Inst. Atmospheric Physics, Beijing, China

Shankman/Horn, *Inside Climate News*

without cost.[*] The capacity of the oceans as a carbon sink, while not given as much attention, is also a key part of the climate-change picture, and in this sense, the oceanic commons is every bit as important a global resource as the atmospheric one.

The issue of climate change is the question of administering global resources so as to avoid a tragedy of the commons that would degrade the Earth's capacity to support life.

---

[*] Climate change skeptics are correct, by the way, when they say there is nothing poisonous about carbon dioxide; it is the natural product of animal respiration; indeed, life depends on it. The problem is not the substance itself, but rather the effects of rapid change in its level of concentration.

Measurement questions

The resource in question here is the capacity of the atmosphere and the oceans to absorb greenhouse gas emissions without causing catastrophic damage. At present, these phenomena are beyond our ability to accurately measure. Emissions of greenhouse gases can be tallied up with relative ease. However, the effects are not the least bit easy to quantify and predict, for they depend on a multiplicity of influences that interact, often in chaotic ways.

Greenhouse gas pollution must be understood in terms of both flows and stocks. The annual amount of CO_2 put into the air is a flow, but the level of CO_2 in the atmosphere at a given time is a stock. The overall greenhouse effect is determined by the stock of greenhouse gas in the atmosphere. Once a pollutant is released into the air, it stays there for a long time. Initially, it was thought that accelerated absorption of carbon dioxide in the oceans would mitigate atmospheric pollution, but in recent years it has become clear that this process is not fast enough to effectively decrease atmospheric warming. Additionally, it contributes to ocean acidification, which sets off another whole suite of ecological problems.

There are many, many complicating factors; we'll just mention a few examples here. CO_2 is the most worrisome greenhouse gas in terms of volume, but it isn't the only one; methane is actually about 30 times more potent at trapping heat. Relatively large amounts of methane are produced by domestic animals, particularly beef cattle. However, global warming itself creates another, potentially far greater, source of methane. Large expanses of permafrost in places like Yukon and Siberia are beginning to thaw — and as they do, they release copious amounts of methane. This is one of many examples of feedback effects that can affect the process of climate change. The melting of sea ice is another. Ice is highly reflective; newly-exposed ocean surface absorbs much more solar energy as heat, which contributes to further melting.

These large-scale phenomena contribute to local effects that are even harder to predict. For example: accelerated melting in the Arctic Ocean has made it newly feasible to develop oil deposits in that region. This has led to more shipping. A more accessible "Northwest passage" has led to even more commercial shipping in the region. Diesel-powered ships emit sooty exhaust which settles on nearby snow, darkening it, making it absorb more heat and melt more quickly.

Ecological shifts attributable to climate change end up having more local effects than anyone could predict. Plants take in CO_2 in their metabolism, so it stands to reason that, all else being equal, plants would benefit from an increase of CO_2 in the air. As it happens, though, this benefits some plants more robustly than others; poison ivy is one such.

In order to stave off runaway climate change, it will be necessary to stabilize the overall stock of greenhouse gases at some safe amount. The current concentration of CO_2 is easily measured.[*] Prior to the industrial revolution, it fluctuated between around 180 parts per million during ice ages, to 280 PPM during interglacial warm periods. Between 1950 and today, the level rose from about 310 PPM to its current level, a bit above 400 PPM. There has never been such a large increase in such a short time. Climate activist Bill McKibben, among others, has argued that 350 PPM is a safe, sustainable plateau level; he named his movement website 350.org for that reason. Climate researcher Nicholas Stern identified 550 PPM as a level above which irreversible catastrophe would be virtually inevitable.[†]

To move toward a desired stock of CO_2 an annual flow target must be arrived at. This would be measured in tons of CO_2 per year, the major sources being transportation, power generation, agriculture and, in a negative sense, the amount of CO_2-absorbing forests or ocean plant life. Part of the process of designing a workable mitigation campaign would be estimating the cost of achieving various levels of reduction. Because there are so many different sources of greenhouse-gas pollution — so many fires burning, as it were — a variety of methods would be used to reduce them. In the most egregious cases, command-and-control methods can be used,

---

[*] While methane, and other greenhouse gases such as fluorocarbons, also contribute, their overall volume is much less. They are part of any comprehensive climate-change model, but our cursory overview can focus on CO_2 as a broad indicator. This is dealt with in the literature by referring to tons of CO_2 *equivalent*. See United States Environmental Protection Agency, *U.S. Greenhouse Gas Inventory Report*

[†] See Stern, "The Economics of Climate Change"

such as simply outlawing new coal-fired power plants, or mandating certain levels of fuel efficiency in cars.

However, it is more efficient to impose a cost on greenhouse gas emissions, creating a market incentive to decrease them as much as possible. The form that this charge should take is a matter of policy debate, informed by principles of equity and efficiency — and, because the cost of effective remedies is likely to rapidly increase over time, political expediency must be one of the criteria. Society may not be able to wait until the very most efficient solution becomes popular.

There are two basic methods of "internalizing" the cost of greenhouse pollution: carbon taxes, and tradable emissions allowances.[‡] The first would set the cost, with a tax on the carbon content of fuels, and then allow the market to determine the level of emissions. On the other hand, a tradable-allowance system, which is commonly referred to as "cap-and-trade," would mandate the maximum permissible level of emissions, and let the market determine the price of the needed reductions by means of tradable credits or permits. Each system has benefits and drawbacks. The cap-and-trade system tends to be more politically palatable — because it is, to some extent, inherently weighted in favor of bigger players who have already done more polluting. The bias is explicit in cases where the cap is based on historical pollution levels: bigger polluters get more credits to trade. Even when permits are auctioned, though, larger, better-established firms can afford more of them.

In the US, in the 1990s, a cap-and-trade system achieved the goal of cost-effectively reducing sulfur dioxide emissions to address the problem of acid rain.[§] The program did not solve the system's inherent equity problems, however; it clearly benefited some large power companies whose pollution allowances were "grandfathered" when it began. This is consistent with the Coase Theorem, which holds that if the overall goal is to decrease a negative externality, it doesn't matter to whom the initial pollution rights are allocated, as long as there is a market incentive to decrease them.

The Georgist ideal is that the value of natural opportunities belongs to the community. Until people are willing to pay for

‡ See Frank, "Pricing Carbon..."

§ See Stavins, "The US sulphur dioxide cap..."

access to land (including the atmospheric commons) it has no market value, and the community has no claim to it. It would appear that the use of the atmosphere as a pollution sink had no value until recently — yet, past greenhouse gas emissions contribute to the present danger. Some people have dumped considerably more than others. Past emission levels correlate strongly with levels of industrial development and standards of living. Despite the fact that they did not understand the potential for harm, it has now become clear that polluters have enjoyed the natural opportunity of using the atmosphere as a pollution sink, at the expense of the whole community. Thus, the imposition of a charge on carbon emissions is justified. Polluters are not due any payment for reducing pollution; instead, they should be compelled to pay a fee, to motivate them to cease the harmful behavior.

Some argue that a pollution tax would be still better. This tax would be based on the actual amount of greenhouse pollution emitted, rather than the carbon content of the fuel. The pollution tax would have efficiency benefits, for it would apply a price directly to the behavior we wish to discourage. Carbon-capture and sequestration (CCS) technology is being developed for power plants and other large industrial applications, and a pollution tax would provide a targeted incentive to develop this technology. Some research is even being done into carbon-scrubbing devices that could be used on individual cars, but this technology is a long way from practical application — not nearly as far along as electric vehicles. Therefore, a carbon tax seems to be the best alternative for the transportation sector, which in the United States makes up some 27% of total emissions.

Dealing with uncertainty

One of the most challenging aspects of the climate change issue is the lack of specific data. Prediction depends on long-range trends that are not understood in detail, and outcomes can be changed by unforeseen influences. For example, the limits of CO_2 absorption in the oceans, and the effects on sea life of the resulting increase in acidification, was not even considered in early climate-change models. We aren't yet able to accurately predict the severity and speed of climate-change effects such as sea-level rise, severe weather, coral bleaching, etc. We are virtually certain that such things will pose significant costs, but we don't know how much they will be or how soon they will come due. These uncertainties make it problematic to arrive at an appropriate baseline for a mitigation policy. Too high a price will burden the economy; too low will fail to achieve sufficient reduction of pollution. There is no way to know for sure.

Nicolaus Tideman and Florence Plassman have proposed a novel strategy for dealing with this problem. They suggest that policymakers survey the range of estimated social costs of emitting a ton of CO_2. Emitters would be required to purchase bonds, per ton of CO_2 that they emit. The price of the bonds would be the highest reasonable estimate of the social cost of the emission. There is a good chance that this price would be overestimated — and it is also likely that the social cost will decline eventually, as overall pollution levels decrease. If that happens, the bonds will acquire a cash value. Prof. Tideman explains the proposal as follows:

> We're not sure how harmful CO_2 is, and we expect our understanding to improve in the next few decades. So we tell emitters, "You need to put up a deposit for as much as it might cost — say $100 per ton. You get a deposit receipt, which you can sell for whatever you can get. In thirty years we will hold a scientific meeting, where the world's best experts make their guess as to what the price should have been. Whoever has the deposit receipt gets the overcharge back, plus interest. If informed people think that in 30 years scientists will guess that the right price is $35, then the deposit receipt sells for $65, and it costs you $35 to emit a ton of CO_2.

Thus, in effect, the carbon tax becomes a futures market. The impossibility of accurately assessing the social cost of greenhouse pollution need not hinder the establishment of an effective carbon tax. There would be some overhead in running the bond market, but there are many efficient futures markets in today's economy. Many people are unwilling to devote resources to solve a problem that may turn out to be less dangerous than was thought. Tideman and Plassman's proposal effectively eliminates that objection.[*]

---

[*] Responding to the concern that his proposed program would create a burdensomely high initial outlay, Prof. Tideman responded, "...a more complex system would deal with your concern. Along with the deposits collected, the government would pass out carbon tax revenue shares to all citizens. The

Different worlds (within the One World)

Every ton of greenhouse gas goes into the same air and causes the same effects. It's everyone's problem — though some places, by accident of geography, will have to endure worse effects, such as low-lying Bangladesh, hurricane-prone Caribbean islands or coastal cities such as Mumbai or Washington DC. Nevertheless, industrial countries have had many years to build up great fortunes and formidable economic advantages, while using the global carbon sink without cost. Even while many kinds of local or regional pollution problems were identified and (to some degree, at least) dealt with, disposal of greenhouse gases was free. Developing nations don't take kindly to being told not to use the fuels that brought prosperity to rich nations. For example, China overtook the United States in 2007 as the world's largest producer of CO_2. The United States continues to produce far more greenhouse pollution per capita — but China has many more people. India's industrial economy is also growing rapidly. These trends show why the problem of climate change must be addressed internationally — and underscore the difficulties to be faced in arriving at a workable program. A poor country with a relatively inefficient economy may use energy very wastefully — and yet, because of its vastly lower overall consumption, may contribute far less to overall greenhouse emissions than a richer country. However, as the example of China shows, the potential of poor nations to transform their economies using the Western industrial model is fraught with danger.

To illustrate some of the counterintuitive dimensions of this, let's consider the energy economy in Africa.[*] In many African countries, reliable fuel for cooking is hard to come by. People use firewood, when they can get it. Until pretty recently, they could gather dead wood, in forests that seemed too big to ever be depleted. However, charcoal, which is wood (preferably hardwood) carbonized by burning in a hot, low-oxygen flame — is a better fuel for cooking. An industry has arisen to provide it. Hardwood trees

---

financial markets would trade both the deposits and the revenue shares. Anyone who owned both a deposit and a revenue share for the payment from the deposit could exchange the two of them for the full amount of the deposit. Thus there would be no need to keep savings in the form of deposits."

[*] See Onishi, "Africa's Charcoal Economy..."

in unregulated forests are logged and burned. This releases CO_2, of course, and also depletes the carbon-sink (and habitat) resource of the forest. The market for charcoal grows as more people leave the countryside and gather in cities, and more people gather in cities as the countryside gets denuded of its forests. Meanwhile, there are abundant reserves of more efficient fuels: in Nigeria, billions of cubic feet of natural gas are burned annually, in continuous flares, the flames of which can be seen from outer space.[†] Obviously natural gas is a much more efficient fuel than charcoal. Yet no one has yet found a way to profitably fund the infrastructure that would allow Nigerian gas to be used. This has much to do with the "resource curse" character of Nigeria's economy: exploitation of its crude oil resources brings easy profits to a privileged few. Nevertheless, to replace African charcoal fuel with natural gas would confer great environmental benefits.

In net terms, however, Africa's energy economy, wasteful as it is, is barely a drop in the climate-change bucket. Africa is the world's most sparsely-populated continent — even counting the vast open spaces of Russia and Canada. Among continents, Africa also has by far the lowest per-capita energy consumption. Charcoal is cheap in Africa precisely because there are still large expanses of forest to chop down and burn. No African country is anywhere near the top tier of greenhouse gas emitters. The entire continent of Africa, population 1.22 billion, emits less CO_2 than India — and much less than the United States.

There is a moral argument that the world's rich nations, having profitably burned all that fossil fuel for all those years, now bear a disproportionate responsibility for the cleanup. But there is a practical argument too: without the rich nations' scientific and technological leadership, it won't get done.

Where's the motivation?

Many, possibly most, people acknowledge that climate change poses a level of risk that calls for an immediate campaign to shift away from fossil fuels. Yet the best we have done so far is the Paris Accord of 2014. This agreement, ratified by 145 nations, represents a groundbreaking acknowledgment of the problem's seriousness.

† See Da Silva, "Where's the Off Switch..."

Yet it has no legally binding provisions for actual pollution abatement. Signatories to the Paris agreement have pledged to set national goals for greenhouse gas reduction, and issue periodic public reports about their progress. They are free to relax those goals as they go, and there is no mechanism to enforce compliance.

Yet, as of June 2017, the Paris accord's tactful suggestions have become too strong for the United States. President Donald Trump has declared himself a proud member of the climate change denial team. Like him, climate change deniers tend to be strongly nationalistic. They favor strong national defense and are suspicious of immigrants. They believe strongly in the threat of terrorist attack and are ready to devote copious resources to guard against it.

We are verging into psychological analysis that's beyond the scope of this essay, but for now, we can suggest a hypothesis: that the climate-change denial movement is based on an essentially sentimental form of nationalism.* Yet climate change is an inherently international issue. It is this cognitive dissonance — rather than any technical difficulty or dispute over facts — that impedes progress. Civilization seems to have entered a watershed moment in the way it understands territory, sovereignty and the fate of the planet. Any effort to remedy this problem must be international. Yet many people simply refuse to accept any form of international sovereignty. Indeed, many Americans believe the *national* government has too much power. This is an element of ideology; for these people, the threat of anthropogenic climate change is literally unthinkable.

This helps to explain why the climate change debate inspires such vehemence on both sides. On the other, "green" side, people shake their fists yelling "The science is irrefutable!" — though they have read none of the science. They have been inspired by the iconic Apollo photograph of the whole Earth. They are appalled by what they see as useless, immoral military conflicts, a waste of good resources on huge stocks of weapons, piled up by nations against other nations. They think "one world" is a fine idea — and they see the global nature of the climate-change problem as fitting organically into that: a direct message from Gaia.

---

* See Collomb, "The Ideology of Climate Change Denial..." and Roberts, "Bannon is Pulling One Over..."

Each side sees the other side's world view as fundamentally flawed.

The power of the big picture

The Georgist vision offers a vital insight into how to bridge this conceptual divide. Georgism asserts the community's right to the value of natural opportunities. In this, it serves to clarify the incessant debate over what should be private and public property. This insight suggests a path toward resolving our seemingly impenetrable debate over global resources.

There are a number of contentious issues that seem intractable, until the "land" (or "natural opportunities") piece of the puzzle is fitted into place. For example: progressive-minded people bitterly oppose the processes of globalization and international trade, seeing how they bring about a "race to the bottom" in which nations seek to attract jobs and investment by removing protections for workers or the environment. When trade agreements facilitate this, they are seen as "eroding national sovereignty." Yet it can be argued that when society cedes the rent of land to private owners, it yields up the most important element of sovereignty.[†] Land rents, which are created by the entire community, are yielded to private interests — often to foreign ones.

The issue of taxation is another of these Gordian knots. To support public services, communities resort to burdensome taxes on productive activity. These taxes make businesses less competitive, exacerbating the "race to the bottom." Indeed, if we don't consider the Georgist remedy, the entire issue of taxation is absurd, because the rent of natural opportunities is demonstrably the first and best (and some say "the only proper") source of public revenue.

Even among people who concur with the climate-change thesis and recognize the dangers, there is a curious lack of urgency about this issue. It would seem that the future serviceability of the planet's air and water is the ultimate "land lssue." Yet even Georgist activists may be tempted to downplay the urgency of climate change. Yes, it's important, but there are only so many hours in a day. It's hard enough to get across the perfectly self-evident idea that a city ought to collect its land rent and stop levying fines on

---

† See Davies, "On National Sovereignty"

workers for working or builders for building. How are we going to sell the notion of some universal right to unpolluted air?

Yet, just as there is only one global atmosphere, perhaps there is only one global Georgist movement, which encompasses (to a greater or lesser degree) everyone who strives toward justice and sustainability. It's very likely that in the long run, we can have neither of those things unless we recognize that the resources of our planet must be shared by all.

This isn't as radical a notion as it may sound at first. It just requires us to expand our field of view. As John Locke famously noted, there is nothing wrong with a person asserting private ownership of a piece of land, as long as there is as much, and as good, land still available for the next person. When that is no longer the case, land rent comes into being — and Georgists believe that land rent rightfully belongs to the community. Once land rent becomes economically important, some form of government arises to administer it. The atmospheric commons is land; the basic principle is the same. Until recently, people could dump as much greenhouse gas into it as they wanted; there was as much good air for the next person. But now a rent has arisen for the atmosphere's carbon-sink services. If history is any guide, some form of government will eventually arise to administer it.

If we take the threat of climate change seriously, then we need to facilitate that development. Establishing a new administrative level need not threaten existing institutions. People have long accepted the simultaneous jurisdiction of multiple sovereign levels. We accept local, regional and national authority in various matters; we vote, and pay taxes, at each level. Nevertheless, the initial establishment of higher levels of government is often controversial. For example, it took some 90 years for the United States to resolve the issue of slavery at the constitutional level — and issues of states' rights remain contentious to this day. The European Union continues to struggle with a wide range of issues, including immigration, defense and taxation. It should surprise no one that establishing an international jurisdiction over global resources would be a challenge, but sometimes hard things need to be done. It seems that we need an international authority if we are going to avoid the catastrophe of unchecked climate change.

Georgists have often focused tactically on one particular aspect of resource rents: local property taxes, land trusts, royalties on extractive resources, etc. It is sensible to focus on a single political avenue. Nevertheless, when we focus on one campaign, we risk missing the big picture. Economically, land is central; it is essential to every form of production.* This is demonstrated by the fact that there are so many ways to come at the public collection of land rents, as exemplified by the essays in this book. It may be, however, that all of those efforts are weakened, if there is no concurrent effort to teach the broad outlines of the Georgist philosophy. By connecting the dots, we can fortify all of our various implementation efforts. After all, why should people accept a global jurisdiction over the atmospheric commons, when they have no such jurisdiction over the vacant lots in their center cities, or the vast acreages held by foreign corporations?

It could be that a broad understanding of the land issue is the missing link in *both* local tax-reform efforts and international climate-change advocacy. It's our land; it's our air and water. We need to see this not simply in sentimental or moral terms but also as effective economic policy. And if that is so, it implies that at this fateful moment in history, the most practically effective work to do is — as Henry George said in 1886 — the work of education. We must explain how land truly is at the base of everything — economically, politically and environmentally. When people clearly understand that, they will know what to do.

---

* This remains true, despite the tendency of the subdiscipline of "land economics" to make it look like a specialty. The economic effects of resource rent are relevant to macroeconomics, public and financial economics — but specialists in these fields tend not to compare notes about it.

Appendix: Excerpts from the original COLT Manual (1971)

National ownership of natural resource lands

Any discussion of federal land policy must assume that there will be no major additions to or disposals from the total acreage of land in federal ownership in the foreseeable future. Since 1931 no official study has recommended major disposals, while all private attempts to this end have been quickly killed in Congress, and according to the authors, "support for additional land is vastly less than for retention of land now owned."

This striking continuity of federal land policy is explained as follows by the former head of the Bureau of Land Management:

1. Many federally owned lands have multiple use potentials which can all be realized only under public ownership; any given private owner would necessarily emphasize only one economic aspect of such lands to the exclusion of others.
2. Public lands provide assured future open space for a variety of public needs in the future.
3. Federal and locally owned lands provide the basis for economic survival of many localities and regions in the Western US, while revenues paid to local governments in lieu of taxes on federal lands provide a large measure of local revenue.
4. Public lands provide a flywheel safety factor to provide jobs to unemployed persons in depressed times and in depressed areas, and at the same time ensure the continued long-term viability of these lands.
5. National defense requirements favor the continue public

ownership of certain fissionable materials, strategic minerals, offshore oil and gas lands, and some timber lands.

6. Many lands are not productive enough to allow private owners to make any income from the lands or to pay taxes on them.

Evolution of the present system of federal land ownership

The history of federal land ownership in the US is divided into five eras, as follows:

1. **Era of acquisition (chiefly 1803-1865).** During this period the US came to extend its boundaries from the original thirteen states to include its whole present continental extent, through a series of cessions from the original states to the United States, purchases from foreign countries, treaties and other arrangements. With the exception of Texas, which joined the Union as an independent republic and retained title to its whole territory, all the rest of the area of the US began as the "public domain" of the federal government.

2. **Era of disposal (chiefly 1815-1930).** In accordance with a then broadly popular public policy, throughout the 19th and early 20th centuries, major programs were carried out under which title to approximately 70%, or roughly 1 billion out of the original 1.46 billion acres of the public domain, passed from the federal government to the states, to railroad and other corporations and to private citizens. Much of this land was disposed of under essentially private laws relating to particular pieces of land, but other large quantities were distributed under general programs as grants to the states at the time of their admission to the Union, under the Homestead Act and as grants to railroads. Although the era of major land disposals continued until about 1930, by 1880 concern was becoming widespread that this policy was not achieving all the ends it was designed to serve. As an example, the census of all farmers were tenants. Proposals for changes in these policies of massive disposal first appeared in the 1870s.

3. **Era of reservation (chiefly 1890-1935).** This era began with the creation of Yellowstone National Park in 1872, and dates in a major way from the authorization by Congress in 1891 of

the creation of a system of forest reserves, or national forests, by presidential proclamation. Other lands were set aside as grazing lands, national parks, watershed and other areas. The remaining land in federal ownership not specifically set aside for any of these particular purposes has come to be known as "unreserved and unappropriated public domain."

4. Era of custodial management (chiefly 1905-1950). This era was characterized by the extensive, or low-intensity, management of the newly reserved lands. It began with the creation of the forest service in 1905, the first efforts of which were directed to fire prevention, control of trespass and positive steps to facilitate use of the lands for grazing, timber harvest, recreation and other uses. In this period, Congress passed laws allowing the purchase of land by the federal government for management purposes, exchange of lands between the government and private citizens, leasing of mineral rights on federal lands, and the creation of grazing districts to be operated as active enterprises.

5. Era of intensive management (chiefly 1950 onwards). This period has been characterized by two new developments in federal land management: a great increase in the amount of capital and labor expended on the federal lands; and a sharp rise in the revenues derived from these lands. In 1951, for the first time, gross cash revenues exceed total direct appropriations for all purposes on all federal lands combined. No legislative act marked the transition from extensive to intensive use of these lands; rather, it was simply a widespread sharp increase in the public demand for the use of all these lands following World War II that ushered in the new era.

In regard to minerals and oil on the public domain, Clawson and Held point out that most of the valuable deposits went into private ownership long ago, and present opportunities on public land are slight. However, in the 1960s vast new oil and mineral resource areas opened up on federal lands: the offshore or continental shelf land; the oil shale deposits in the Rocky Mountain plateau areas of Colorado, Wyoming and Utah. (The immense oil discoveries in the Northern slope of Alaska were on state lands.)

In the case of offshore lands, both international and national court decisions have firmly established the federal government as the primary owner of these resources against state governments and other national governments. In the 1950s it was estimated that US offshore areas contained oil reserves of up to 100 billion barrels. It is expected that the federal government will retain close control over these rights, not squandering them as it did others in the past.

Factors influencing federal land policy

The American public influences federal land management policies in two ways: by the direct actions of individuals, such as visiting parks and applying for leases; and by the lobbying of various organizations, professional, semiprofessional, public, industry and research groups, in the areas of forestry, grazing, minerals, petroleum, recreation and conservation. Clawson and Held felt that the various lobbies are sufficiently strong to block most bills that are contrary to the interests they represent, but no one lobby is strong enough to secure passage of a bill that it alone favors. Most major steps forward have been achieved only when the general public has been made interested and aroused over a particular, usually oversimplified issue.

Within the government, the budget of the federal land managing agencies go through the same states of executive and legislative review as do those of other agencies. This system has two major drawbacks as it applies to the federal lands: 1) the basic philosophy is wrong in that it regards land management as a general government expense when it is in fact a wealth-creating activity. Spending or investment should be determined by the resulting productivity of federal lands, not simply by the amount of funds "available"; 2) the budget allows no carryover of funds from one year to the next and thus allows no flexibility in spending over the period of greatest activity, the summer months June and July, when one fiscal year ends and another begins.

Dealings between citizens competing for the use of federal lands and the various managing agencies have in general depended very little on competitive market forces, but rather on administrative decisions based on the traditional goals of encouraging maximum access and production.

This policy of administrative price-setting has advantages and disadvantages. Among the advantages are: 1) socially desirable but non-revenue producing functions are preserved; 2) multiple-use management of specific tracts of land can be assured; 3) economic protection may be provided for small vulnerable interests as against larger more powerful ones.

Among the disadvantages are: 1) the process is more complicated than one based simply on awarding each tract to the highest bidder; 2) it increases the need for appeal and review procedures; 3) it is more open to political pressures. In general, as more bidders become interested in using federal grazing, forestry and mineral lands, more competitive pricing processes will result. Mineral and petroleum leases are sold on the basis of a cash bonus bid over a fixed royalty, usually 12½% to 25% of gross revenue.

Goals and means to goals

Some goals of federal land policy are as follows:

a. In the case of timber, mineral, petroleum and grazing lands which produce a saleable product, maximization of the output of that product is an appropriate goal.
b. In the case of recreational, scenic, watershed, wildlife and other aspects of federal land operations that have no readily identifiable market value, an appropriate goal is maximization of the public access to and enjoyment of these lands.
c. In either of the above cases, maximum efficiency, the method of increasing investment until marginal expenditures or costs begin to exceed marginal revenues or benefits, should be the basic guiding principle, as in private enterprise. With regard to the recreational and other non-monetary aspects of federal land management, the intensity of management of federal lands should be governed by the public interest.
d. In the case of federal lands that yield saleable products, it is an appropriate goal to seek these lands, at least in cases where this goal does not conflict with more important goals. At the same time, while no excessive burdens should be placed on local government units because of their proximity to federal lands, there appears to be no reason to limit or alter the use of these lands for the exclusive benefit of a local governmental unit.

Special Land Uses — Franchises, Air Rights, Etc.

Besides the use of land for commercial and residential purposes, and the extraction of natural resources, there are uses of land which require access to a special aspect or portion of land while it may continue to be used in ordinary ways. Such are public utilities (electricity, gas, telephone, telegraph) which require use of public ways for their service lines. These usually operate under franchises.

Air rights involve the right, literally, to build in the air over land already used for a purpose that does not require building upward, such as a railroad. Easements, such as rights of way, exist where one party has to use a portion of another party's land, e.g., in order to have access to a public thoroughfare, or to other facilities, such as water supply.

The use of air waves by radio and television are also partial monopolies in the sense that a particular frequency has to be assigned to a particular broadcasting station. Tax exemption of property used for a special purpose, usually nonprofit, educational, etc., is also a privilege, one that presupposes a contribution to society.

Franchises

A franchise is a special privilege extended to individuals or companies to serve the public in a special capacity with the aid of public facilities. The privilege granted is usually exclusive. Franchises are most commonly granted to public utilities, such as gas and electric companies.

Because a franchise is usually exclusive, it has a monopoly value. Just as the value of land is not created by the landowner, so the value of the franchise is not created by those who hold them. Rather, the franchise value is created and maintained by the community and should be collected by the community. As a monopoly, a franchise value is thus the capitalized value of the franchise while leaving to the franchise holder such earnings as are due to his capital.

A number of methods have been proposed to collect the franchise value for the community. Among them are the taxation of the franchise value as capitalized excess earnings, taxation of the annual earnings of the franchise, and competitive bidding.

The value of the franchise depends upon its capacity to generate a return on investment greater than that which can be obtained in other enterprises. The earnings of public utilities, the most common form of franchises, are determined by the rates they charge and the services they render. Under modern regulatory practice, rates and services are regulated so as to keep the earnings of public utilities at a fair and normal level. As a consequence, there would be no excess earnings and the franchise would have no value.

A parcel of land is subject to the competition of other parcels in determining its value. A franchise as a single unit in a particular community is not subject to the competition of similar units. Therefore, a tax levied on the franchise (as well as on the tangible property) will reduce or destroy its market value. Regulation, however, destroys not only the capital value of the franchise but also the rental value, since it would so reduce the rates and increase the service requirements that the rates charged by the utility would be at or near cost. Rather than appropriate the franchise value for the community, regulation destroys it. Thus there is a conflict between the taxation and the regulation of public utilities. If a company has excessive earnings, an increase in tax payments would divert the earnings to revenue and thus benefit taxpayers rather than benefiting consumers through lower rates.

Easements

Real property is actually composed of many different property rights. The owner of these, called the fee owner, can transfer any of these rights to another party. One of the ways of making such a transfer is the grant of an easement, which is simply the right or privilege a person has acquired in another's land. Usually an easement is granted in the form of a deed and, unless there is a reversionary clause, is granted in perpetuity. There are three major classes of easements: subsurface easements, such as for pipelines, underground utility lines and storm drains; surface easements, such as flowage easements, and rights of way for electric transmission lines and avocational rights of way.

An easement grant creates two new estates within the easement area. The first estate may be either an easement appurtenant or an easement in gross. An easement appurtenant is one that is created for, or does benefit to, the easement holder in the use of land owned by him. An example is an easement for a road through a tract of land adjoining the easement holder's land increasing access to and from his land. The easement is attached to the land of the easement holder; the tract of land that benefits from the easement is known as the dominant estate. An easement in gross is one that is not created or does not benefit any land owned by the easement holder. Examples of this are pipeline and flowage easements. Rather than being attached to any land owned by the easement holder, the easement is attached to the grantee, whether it be an individual, a corporation or a government agency.

The other estate created by an easement grant is the landowner's property rights remaining within the easements area. The property rights retained by the owner are commonly called the underlying fee of the easement. The easement holder acquires only those rights that are conveyed in the deed, express or implied, plus the secondary right to do whatever is reasonably necessary for the full enjoyment of the grant. All other rights remain with the fee owner and he may use them as long as their use does not interfere with the use granted in the easement. The amount and kind of rights retained by the grantor vary greatly, but some examples are the right to grow crops on the land surface, mineral and oil rights, and the right to grant other easements on the same tract providing they are not inconsistent with the use of the original easement.

The general approach to the valuation of the easements is as follows: the market value of the parcel from which the easement is acquired is first determined. This parcel is commonly called the larger parcel. From this value the market value of the full fee of the easement area (considered as a portion of the larger parcel before the easement is granted) is developed. In many cases there may be more than one type of land use in the easement area as well as in the larger parcel. Since each use will probably have a different market value, an accurate land classification of the easement area will have to be made. Once the market value of the full fee of the easement area is determined, it can be allocated between the market value of the easement and the market value of the underlying fee. This is usually done by subtracting from the market value of the full fee the market value of the underlying fee. In computing the latter, adjustments have to be made for any effects the granting of the easement may have on the market value of the land within the easement area. For example, the granting of an easement for the construction of an underground utility through an orchard would result in the destruction of the trees and the conversion of the land to another use. The market value of the land would reflect these changes. In addition, the need to repair and maintain the line would require tearing up the soil and destroying any crops grown on the land. The resulting loss in efficiency in the use of the land would further reduce its value for agriculture.

An easement or the improvement constructed within it may cause damages to the land in the larger parcel that is located outside the easement area; this land is commonly called the remainder. Any damages to the remainder would be reflected in its market value. Remainder lands will be damaged if the easement interferes with its highest and best use. For instance, an easement may be so located in the larger parcel that the remainder may be too irregular in shape to be used for its supposed highest and best use. The market value of the underlying fee when added to that of the remainder after the easement was exercised equals the market value of the entire property rights owned by the fee owner.

An example of a surface easement is a flowage easement. This is "a right in land acquired by one party through purchase or condemnation from the owner of the fee title to flood the land by artificial means... for various purposes... the use of said land to prevent existence thereon of habitable or use structure and grating access and right over said land for management purposes."* Flowage easements are used in conjunction with flood control projects, water power reservoir projects, navigation dams, soil conservation and irrigation installations, and municipal reservoirs.

The use of the flowage easement varies with natural conditions and with the type of project. For reservoirs, flowage easements are best adapted to wide river valleys with gentle slopes; where the valley slopes are steep and the river current swift, fee acquisition is usually preferable. Where the project is a flood control dam without a permanent pool or a navigation dam or reservoir, usually the entire land is acquired as a flowage easement. In the case of hydroelectric reservoirs and flood control reservoirs with a permanent pool, the land is usually acquired in fee up to the level where the frequency

---

* See Brownell, "The Valuation of Pipeline Easements"

of flooding renders farming impractical. The Corps of Engineers and the Reclamation Service of the Department of Interior set this elevation at the level where flooding occurs every five years (five-year flood frequency line). Above that level, where flooding is less frequent, flowage easements are acquired. Flood frequency charts have been drawn which project the frequency that flooding are preferred to fee acquisition where conditions warrant this method. In most instances, much of the agricultural utility and much of the mineral value of the land remains. The land stays on the tax rolls of state and county governments and there is less disruption of the local economy. Finally, they cost less than acquiring the full fee.

Air Rights

In recent decades there has been an increasing use of air rights as sites for the construction of office building and other types of structures. The most famous and most valuable air rights development is that built over the tracks of the New York Central Railroad in New York City. Starting in 1902, the area north of Grand Central Station witnessed the creation of Park Avenue and the construction of 18 apartment houses, office buildings and hotels, including the Waldorf-Astoria, the Biltmore and the Commodore, the Graybar Building, and most recently, the huge Pan Am (now Met Life) Building erected over Grand Central Station itself.

In 1968, the new Madison Square Garden complex was completed; it occupies the air space over Pennsylvania Station. Chicago probably has the second largest number of air rights developments, including the Central Post Office, the Prudential Building, the twin Marina City apartment towers, and the Merchandise Mart, all built over railroad tracks or freight yards. Other air rights structures have been built in Philadelphia, Pittsburgh, Boston and El Paso. It has been proposed that because of the scarcity of centrally located building sites, middle and low income housing be built over expressways, bridge and tunnel approaches, piers and subway and railroad tracks. Combination school and office or apartment buildings are planned for New York City. The school will occupy the first few floors of the building while offices or apartments would occupy the air space over the school. The owner of the office building or apartment house would be charged for the use of the air rights; the payment would finance the construction of the school, and in many cases, yield surplus funds.

Various social and economic forces have brought the possibility of utilizing air rights for construction purposes to the attention of real estate developers. Downtown land is already highly developed, leaving little vacant land for building. In the past, there was a high rate of demolition of old buildings to prepare sites for new construction. This high rate was due to the steady increase in the value of downtown land, which prompted developers to use the land more intensively so as to exploit the land value to its highest and best use. In recent years, however,[†] downtown land values have in general stagnated. Zoning restrictions, particularly the floor-area ratio which limits the amount of floor space to a specified multiple of the land area, has required the use of larger and larger parcels to erect building equivalent in bulk to past buildings. The ownership pattern of downtown land, where much of the land is divided among small owners, creates the problem of assembling enough parcels to form a parcel large enough to satisfy the zoning regulations. All these factors have forced builders to look for new areas; airspace, particularly the airspace over extensive railroad tracks and freight yards, is one of the answers.

Four major types of air rights agreements have evolved over the years:

1. The leasing of the air rights above the established plane (the air plane) and the air and ground space needed for the foundations of the structure. The lease is for a stipulated period reflecting the economic life of the building and usually carries renewal options. An example of this type is the Park Avenue air rights development.
2. The sale of the air space above a determined air plane with easement rights granted for the construction of caissons and supporting columns through the fee below the plane. Examples of this are the Chicago Post Office Building and the Chicago Union Station.
3. The sale of the fee of the entire property with easements reserved to the seller of surface rights for the operation of the railroad or for other use. The Chicago Sun-Times property is an example.

---

† As of 1971

4. The subdivision method whereby parcels of land and air are sold by the fee owner. The land is subdivided into lots, for bellout supports, caissons, boiler, engine and air-condition machinery rooms, and elevator pits. The airspace is subdivided into lots, for supporting columns, wind-bracing supports, perimeter walls below the air plane (if any), and the building above the plane. Projects that used this approach include the Merchandise Mart and the Prudential Building, both in Chicago. In the latter project, 663 lots were created. The kinds of lots created vary with the construction requirements of the building.

One approach to the valuation of air rights is to treat the air rights parcel as if it were comparable to other parcels of urban land. This is done by hypothesizing an imaginary platform at the level where the air rights holder secures possession of the air rights. In many cases there may be a real concrete platform built over the railroad tracks. The real or imaginary platform is considered a parcel of land which the appraiser can compare with the sales of other parcels in the area to estimate its market value. The value is not, of course, equivalent to the air rights value because an air rights development is not comparable to developments on ground parcels in three respects: there are additional costs, there are limitations on ownership, and there are special problems of accessibility.

The additional cost of an air rights project must be subtracted from the estimated value of the platform. The additional cost arises from, for example, the need to bridge the railroad tracks, the inflexibility of the location of the foundation structures, the operation of the railroad during construction, the unnatural elevation of the building which results in unrentable space between the platforms and the ground, the possible need to construct a new ground level around the building, and the additional legal, engineering, architectural and appraisal fees. The costs will vary with the specific project and thus the valuation must be made in terms of the particular development. If there is no structure in the airspace, the rights can be valued by hypothesizing several buildings indicating the highest and best use with detailed cost assumptions and analyses.

An air rights owner is under some handicaps, regardless of the form of the agreement. First, the owner has little flexibility in regard to the future use of the property. Air rights are usually purchased with a specific project in view; the conditions under which the air rights are purchased or leased are guided by the requirements and restrictions of the particular development. Thus the agreement may not accord with a future development or redevelopment. This problem is handled by amortizing the land value of the platform over the life of the development.

Finally, the problem of accessibility results in another cost that must be deducted from the value of the platform. A platform above railroad trackage has only limited access from the street. Special facilities, such as escalators or ramps, or the rebuilding of a section of the street may be needed. The cost of doing this must be taken into account in the valuation process.

To summarize this approach, the value of the real or imaginary platform, considered as a parcel of land, is estimated by means of the comparative sales method. From this value is deducted the costs resulting from limited accessibility, the various disadvantages of ownership, and the additional costs as compared to a development built on the ground. The value thus arrived at is the market value of air rights.

A different approach, taken by Hall, Harper and Leyden is the actual appraisal they made in 1952 of the air rights of the Prudential Building in Chicago. They regard the value of the air rights as a residual value of the entire fee rights of the land. First the market value of the complete fee rights of the parcel on which the building is located is determined. From this value is deducted the additional costs and the losses incurred by the air rights developer as compared to a ground level development on the same site. The result yields the market value of the air rights.

Air Waves

One of the most valuable resources that should not be overlooked is the air waves utilized for broadcasting purposes. Their public nature is officially recognized in the basic law governing the radio and television industry, the Communications Act of 1934: "It is the purpose of the Act, among other things, to maintain control of the United States over all the channels of interstate and foreign radio transmission, and to *provide for the use of such channels, but not the ownership thereof,* by persons for limited periods of time, under licenses granted by Federal authority, and no such license shall be construed to create any rights beyond the terms, conditions and period of the license." (Section 301; emphasis added.)

In addition, licensees must sign a waiver of any claims to the use of any particular frequency as against the regulatory power of the United States government because of previous use of that frequency (Section 304).

By international agreement, the frequencies of that part of the electromagnetic spectrum devoted to communications have been allocated in the following bands:

> **10 – 535 kilocycles: radio telegraph and radio beacons used by ships and aircraft**
>
> **535 – 1605 kilocycles: standard (AM) broadcast**
>
> **1605 kc. – 25 megacycles: long distance radio telegraph and telephone, ships at sea, planes in air, international broadcasting**
>
> **25 – 890 megacycles: public safety, citizens radio, land transportation, industrial**
>
> **88 – 108 mc.: FM broadcast**
>
> **54 – 216 mc.: Very High Frequency (VHF) Television**
>
> **470 – 890 mc.: Ultra High Frequency (UHF) Television (Channels 14 – 830**
>
> **890 – 30,000 mc.: radio navigation, common carrier and mobile services, and other specialized radio services**
>
> **30,000 – 300,000 mc.: experimental purposes**

The Federal Communications Commission is empowered to allocate or to designate specific bands of the spectrum to specific communication services, and to assign, i.e., to permit a station to provide services on a specific channel at a specific location.

Each channel in the electromagnetic spectrum possesses an inherent monopoly value just as each parcel of land does. Each license is an exclusive privilege to use a particular channel in a particular community. As the rent of land should be collected by the community, so the value of each frequency channel could be collected by the community.[‡]

[‡] For an updated description of broadcast frequencies and their valuation, see Randolph, "Tuning in to Spectrum Valuation"

Tax Exemption

The principle behind tax exemption is that the persons or organizations exempted from taxation are rendering to the community a valuable service, and this service is a contribution in lieu of taxes. Traditionally, religious, education, charitable, and nonprofit organizations have been exempted from property taxation, as well as from income taxes and other forms of taxes. Government property is tax-exempt, as are foreign consulates and embassies.

Ordinarily, only property that is used for the purposes of the organizations is legitimately tax-exempt. If a tax-exempt institution owns property that it rents out commercially, such property should be taxed. A famous example is Radio City in New York, which is owned by Columbia University but on which taxes are paid. An exception to this rule is property owned by the Cooper Union for the Advancement of Science and Art. All its property is exempt, including that rented out for commercial purposes. This is due to a special law passed in 1859 specifically giving Cooper Union this privilege. A notable example of Cooper Union property is the Chrysler Building, an extremely valuable property which pays no taxes. This situation has been criticized and contested, but so far the law has stood; it is, however, an exceptional case.

Since tax exemption is a privilege, under a system of land value taxation, the value of the service rendered by the tax-exempt organization should bear a relation to the value of the land it is using; the service it gives to the community should be construed as at least equal in value to the rent it would otherwise pay to the community.

Some Georgists believe that tax exemption should be done away with altogether under a system of land value taxation. Some non-Georgists also want to abolish tax exemption, especially with respect to churches, on the grounds that it violates separation of church and state, and that is also infringes on equal constitutional rights. However, tax exemption has been tested in the courts and has held up in cases where the property is being used for the purposes for which exemption was granted. But courts have agreed that properties owned by tax-exempt institutions and used for profit and commercial purposes may be subject to taxation.

International ownership of natural resource land

In 1966, a serious suggestion was made by the United Nations Association of the USA that the General Assembly of the UN declare the title of the international community to the high seas beyond the continental shelves, and to outer space, and that it establish appropriate administrative arrangements to manage this title.

We shall accordingly review here something of the context of the international law of the sea, of which such proposals form a part, and also some indications of the coming problems of outer space.

McDougal and Burke postulate, "from the perspective of observers who identify with the whole of mankind," that the chief goal of an international law of the sea is achieving of the greatest good for the greatest number. This goal is best achieved by the following three principles: Firstly, preserving, in as many situations as possible, the inclusive claims of all nations to unrestricted freedom in all uses of the sea. Secondly, honoring certain claims of coastal states to exclusive authority over certain coastal waters, for the sake of (a) protecting the coastal state from threats to its security, (b) regulating such activities as sanitation, conservation and the smuggling of goods or persons, or (c) allowing coastal states to exploit special opportunities stemming from their closeness to particular resources. Thirdly, rejecting excessive claims of individual nations that are not justified by circumstances or that represent encroachments on the community interest. For the application of these principles the authors describe the processes of interaction of states and persons on the oceans, of assertion of claims, and of authoritative decision-making in legal disputes. They emphasize the great importance, for both small and large states, of fostering the growth of international law, rather than flouting it. For "in trials of strength in devouring mankind's common heritage it can only be expected that, while everybody loses, the larger states will emerge the fatter."

Specific legal disputes involving the seas generally deal with some activity within one of the six classic areas of the seas, or they deal with arguments over the precise boundaries between these areas. The six areas are:

Inland water. These are waters such as lakes, rivers or canals that lie wholly within a state. Sovereignty over these waters is of course that of the surrounding state and these waters are not involved in international law.

Internal waters. This category refers to basins such as bays, estuaries or mouths of rivers which lie along the coast but within the baseline (legal version of the coastline) of the state. Sovereignty is again that of the surrounding state, but international law recognizes, for example, the right of ships of any nation to seek shelter from storms in any country's internal waters.

Territorial waters. The territorial sea of a coastal state is the strip of ocean from three to twelve miles wide lying adjacent to its shores; the precise width is still unsettled in international law. Sovereignty over these waters is that of the adjacent state, and includes exclusive rights to mineral and animal resources, authority to regulate navigation in the zone, power to forbid air navigation in the airspace above, authority to regulate sanitation, conservation, smuggling and belligerent use, and other prerogatives. However, a right of innocent passage of vessels of any state is generally recognized in these waters.

Contiguous zones. These are also zones lying just offshore of coastal states, but they are much less precisely defined than are territorial waters. These zones have been incorporated into maritime legal practice in order to allow individual states to exert specific, temporary and limited powers, over particular segments of their offshore waters for particular purposes. Examples would be suppression of hostile weapons shipments, exploitation of continental shelf resources, and missile launching activities.

Continental shelf. This term refers to the area of ocean floor next to coastal states up to the boundary defined by a sharp increase in the slope of the seabed which marks the beginning of the deep sea. The shelf is present around all continents and islands, but its edge may lie anywhere from 10 to 300 miles offshore, and at a depth of 100 to 200 meters. The continental shelves are of interest because of the presence of two types of resources: vast quantities of oil and other mineral deposits whose extraction has been feasible only since about 1950; and sedentary animal species such as shrimp, oysters, pearl shell and others closely associated with the seabed. On the basis of both economic and security considerations, international law has come to recognize the exclusive right of the coastal state to exploitation of the mineral resources of the shelves, but policy concerning the sedentary animal species remains unsettled. Free access is still allowed to all states to extract free-swimming species from the waters overlying the shelves.

High seas. These include all parts of the oceans not coming under any of the above classifications. These areas are subject to little or no jurisdiction, but are freely accessible to all persons or states for such purposes as navigation, laying cables or pipelines, extraction of fish or minerals, basic research or weapon development, or any other as yet unforeseen uses. It is these waters that have been the subject of proposals for internationalization.

McDougal and Burke frequently emphasize the importance of their first principle, of presumptively favoring the common or inclusive right of all nations to any use of the seas in the absence of compelling reasons justifying exclusive claims of particular states. However, the history, not only of the oceans, but of the English commons, of the American public domain and that of many other lands, demonstrates that unless a public interest is actively protected, it tends rapidly to be sold, lost or frankly plundered by private parties or states. Anticipating this course of events, the United Nations Association of the USA proposed in 1966, as noted above, that the UN declare the title of all mankind to the high seas and to outer space, and that it set up appropriate machinery to administer this title. In more detail the goals they hope to achieve are:

1. To avoid controversy among nations arising from conflicting claims to, and appropriative uses of, the uncommitted areas of the earth and its surrounding space – e.g., for fishing rights, and for atmospheric and oceanic nuclear testing.

2. To ensure the most effective economic use of the natural resources of the sea and of outer space. These include fish, minerals, plant life and radio spectrum frequencies. As an example of present abuse in the absence of controls, one species of Antarctic whale

is near extinction due to excessive hunting.

3. To prohibit military use, including the testing of conventional or nuclear weapons.

4. To avoid contamination. This includes contamination of the moon and other planets as well as radioactive and chemical poisoning of the atmosphere and the high seas.

5. To ensure that all nations will be able directly or indirectly to profit by the opportunities and potential resources of these vast areas. This goal embodies the principle that the land belongs to all mankind despite the national differences in technological advancement.

6. To provide the UN with an independent source of income. The present limitations on both the peace-keeping and the international development functions of the UN stem in large part from the refusal of member states to pay for these activities. An independent income for the UN would facilitate both these functions.

Specific steps suggested toward implementing this policy include the following:

1. There should be established a special agency of the United Nations to be called the UN Marine Resources Agency. It should control and administer international marine resources, hold ownership rights, and grant, lease or use these rights in the most economic and efficient manner. It should function with the independence and efficiency of the International Bank, but should distribute its revenues according to the policies and directions of the General Assembly.

2. Whatever UN agency is set up to administer these resources should take steps toward, and see agreement on, revision of the Convention of the Continental Shelf, in order to specify in a non-ambiguous manner the geographic distinction between the continental shelf and the deep sea, with respect to the seabed and the minerals in and on it. The present Convention is very vague, in declaring that the continental shelf extends "out to the 200-meter depth line or beyond that limit to where the depth of superjacent waters admits of the exploitation of the natural resources of the said areas." This phrasing encourages

unilateral claims to the seabed.

3. The General Assembly should declare that the deep sea and the seabed must not be used by nations as an environment in which to install or operate weapons, or for purposes intended to further research on potential weapons or their development. Two precedents exist for such a declaration: 1) in the Antarctic Treaty of December 1959, thirteen governments, including the USA and USSR agreed that Antarctica shall be used for peaceful purposes only, and that military personnel or equipment may be used for scientific research or for peaceful purposes only; 2) the General Assembly in 1963 called upon all states "to refrain from placing in orbit around the earth any objects carrying nuclear weapons or any other kinds of weapons of mass destruction, installing such weapons on celestial bodies, or stationing such weapons in outer space in any other manner."

The chief economic consideration with which we are concerned is that expressed in Goal No. 6 of the UNA-USA, as noted above; i.e., the providing of revenue for the UN from the ocean, other uncommitted portions of the earth, and possibly outer space.

As yet, no "rent" has arisen on the high seas. In order for there to be an economic rent, there must be competing users bidding for a resource in limited supply. Of course, such a situation also assumes an authority to whom the rent is paid, otherwise the competition is settled by war. Although the situation has not arisen for most of the high seas, it is none too soon to settle this question. There has been a rapid proliferation of unilateral claims to continental shelves as these have become technically accessible. There has been acute competition among nations for access to oil deposits found in the North Sea. The just claims of mankind must be considered. Nor should such deliberations become solely legalistic, as has been the tendency with such discussions in the United Nations, but the common right to the bounty of the common property must be recognized and implemented.

With respect to outer space, the UN General Assembly adopted a resolution in 1963, stating, in part: "Outer space and celestial bodies are not subject to national appropriation by claims of sovereignty, by means of use or occupation, or by any other means."

In 1966 the Outer Space Treaty was adopted by the USA, the USSR and other nations, incorporating the above resolution and further specifying the outer space and celestial bodies shall be used exclusively for peaceful purposes.

Much study is being made in the UN and by international law experts on the legal aspects of outer space, but so far very little attention has been paid to possible economic aspects. While no nation is supposed to claim any celestial body, there is still the question of landing on such bodies, establishing observation posts, etc., and no provision has been worked out as to the terms of such tenure. The same principles ought to apply as with any other vast natural resource.

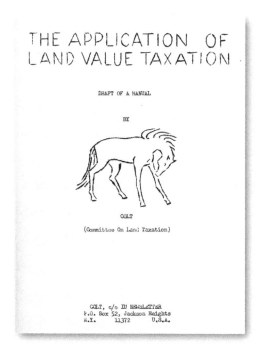

THE APPLICATION OF
LAND VALUE TAXATION

DRAFT OF A MANUAL

BY

COLT

(Committee On Land Taxation)

COLT, c/o IU NEWSLETTER
P.O. Box 52, Jackson Heights
N.Y.   11372   U.S.A.

Works Cited

Andelson, Robert, Ed., *Land Value Taxation Around the World*, 2000, Hoboken, NJ, Wiley-Blackwell

Batt, William, Afterword to Tucker, Gilbert, *The Self-Supporting City*, New York, Robert Schalkenbach Foundation, 2010

Blumgart, Jake, "How Bernie Sanders Made Burlington Affordable", *Slate*, http://www.slate.com/articles/business/metropolis/2016/01/bernie_sanders_made_burlington_s_land_trust_possible_it_s_still_an_innovative.html

Brownell, Keith, "Valuation of Pipeline Easements" *The Appraisal Journal*, April, 1958

Clawson, Marion and Held, Burnell, *The Federal Lands: Their Use and Management*, University of Nebraska Press, 1957

Collomb, Jan-Daniel, The Ideology of Climate Change Denial in the United States, *European Journal of American Studies*, Spring 2014

Commons, John R., "Institutional Economics", *American Economic Review*, vol. 21 (1931), pp. 648-657

Da Silva, Guilherme, "Where's the off switch for Nigerian energy waste?" Earth Journalism Network, http://earthjournalism.net/stories/where2019s-the-off-switch-for-nigerian-energy-waste

Davies, Lindy, "On National Sovereignty", *Georgist Journal* Number 124, Autumn, 2014, http://www.georgistjournal.org/2015/06/01/on-national-sovereignty/

Rent as Public Revenue

Dwyer, Terry, The Taxable Capacity of Australian Land and Resources, *Australian Tax Forum*, Vol.18, No.1, 2003

Einhorn, Robin L., *American Taxation, American Slavery*, Chicago, University of Chicago Press, 2006

Einhorn, Robin L., Species of Property: The American Property-Tax Uniformity Clauses Reconsidered, *The Journal of Economic History*, Vol. 61, No. 4 (Dec., 2001), pp. 974-1008

Fitzgerald, Karl, *Total Resource Rents of Australia*, Melbourne, Prosper Australia. 2013

Foldvary, Fred. "The Business Cycle: A Georgist-Austrian Synthesis." *American Journal of Economics and Sociology*, Vol. 56, No. 4, (October 1997), pp. 521-541.

Frank, Charles, "Pricing Carbon: A Carbon Tax or Cap-And-Trade?", Brookins Institution blog, https://www.brookings.edu/blog/planetpolicy/2014/08/12/pricing-carbon-a-carbon-tax-or-cap-and-trade/

Gaffney, Mason, *After the Crash: Designing a Depression-Free Economy*, Hoboken, NJ, Wiley-Blackwell , 2009

Gaffney, Mason, "Neoclassical Economics as a Strategy Against Henry George" in *The Corruption of Economics*, London, Shepheard-Walwyn, 1994

Gaffney, Mason, *New Life in Old Cities*, New York, Robert Schalkenbach Foundation, 2014

Gaffney Mason, "Oil and Gas: the Unfinished Tax Reform" A paper presented to annual conference of TRED, Cambridge MA, Sept. 1982, pp. 1-53. Available at www.masongaffney.org

George Henry, *Progress and Poverty*, New York, Robert Schalkenbach Foundation, 1879, 1979

George, Henry, *Protection or Free Trade*, New York, Robert Schalkenbach Foundation, 1886, 1980

152

German, Robinson & Youngman, Traditional Methods and New Approaches to Land Valuation, *Land Lines*, Lincoln Institute of Land Policy, July, 2000

Global Carbon Project, *Global Carbon Atlas*, http://www.globalcarbonatlas.org/en/CO2-emissions, 2016

Gwartney, Ted, "Land Assessment for Socializing Land Rent While Untaxing Production", Annual World Bank Conference on Land and Poverty, Washington DC, March 24-27, 2014

Gwartney, Ted, "Land Rents As A Sustainable Revenue Base For China", *Journal of Translation from Foreign Literature of Economics*, http://se.xmu.edu.cn/jzyc/ (2013)

Hall, Arthur, Harper, Harry and Leyden, Richard, "Approaches to the Valuation of Air Rights", *The Appraisal Journal*, July, 1956

Harrison Fred, *The Power in the Land*, London, Shepjeard-Walwyn, 1983

Harrison, Fred, Ed., *The Losses of Nations*, London, Othila Press, 1998

Harrison, Fred, *Wheels of Fortune: Self-funding Infrastructure and the Free Market Case for a Land Tax*, London, Institute of Economic Affairs, 2006

Intergovernmental Panel on Climate Change, *Climate Change 2013: the Physical Science* Basis, http://www.ipcc.ch/report/ar5/wg1/

Kavanagh, Bryan, "The riches-of-oz." The Land Values Research Group, http://lvrg.org.au/files/riches-of-oz.pdf, 2007

Larson, William, New Estimates of Value of Land of the United States, US Bureau of Economic Analysis, 2015, https://www.bea.gov/papers/pdf/new-estimates-of-value-of-land-of-the-united-states-larson.pdf

Lefmann, Ole & Larsen, Karsten, "Denmark" in *Land Value Taxation Around the World*, 2nd edition, Robert Schalkenbach Foundation, 1997

Marshall, John, Johnson v. M'Intosh (1823) http://caselaw.findlaw.com/us-supreme-court/21/391.html

McDougal, Myres and Burke, William, *The Public Order of the Oceans: A Contemporary International Law of the Sea*, Yale University Press, 1952

Oates, Wallace and Schwab, Robert, The Impact of Urban Land Taxation: The Pittsburgh Experience, *National Tax Journal*, Vol. 50, No. 1 (1997) pp.1-21

Onishi, Norimitsu, "Africa's Charcoal Economy is Cooking. The Trees are Paying, *New York Times, June 25, 2016* https://www.nytimes.com/2016/06/26/world/africa/africas-charcoal-economy-is-cooking-the-trees-are-paying.html

Polanyi, Karl, (1944) *The Great Transformation,* New York, Toronto, Farrar & Rinehart, Inc.

Poterba, James, Venture Capital and Capital Gains Taxation, 1989, National Bureau of Economic Research, http://www.nber.org/papers/w2832

Purdy, Lawson, "Municipal Taxation", *Public Policy,* May 14, 1904, http://cooperative-individualism.org/purdy-lawson_municipal-taxation-1904.htm

Purves, Andrew, *No Debt; High Growth; Low Tax — Hong Kong's Economic Miracle Explained,* London, Shepheard-Walwyn, 2015

Randolph, Kim, "Tuning In to Spectrum Valuation", Stout Services, https://www.stoutadvisory.com/insights/article/sj17-tuning-in-to-spectrum-valuation, May 2017

Riley, Don, *Taken for a Ride*, London, Centre for Land Policy Studies, 2001

Roberts, David, "Bannon is pulling one over on Trump. There is zero reason to exit the Paris climate accord." https://www.vox.com/energy-and-environment/2017/5/7/15554286/paris-climate-accord-exit-bannon

Pollock, Walter and Scholz, Karl, *The Science and Practice of Urban Land Valuation : An Exposition of the Somers Unit System*, Philadelphia, Pa., Manufacturers' Appraisal Company, 1926

Shankman, Sabrina and Horn, Paul, "The Most Powerful Evidence Climate Scientists Have of Global Warming", *Inside Climate News*, https://insideclimatenews.org/news/03102017/infographic-ocean-heat-powerful-climate-change-evidence-global-warming

Stavins, Robert, *et. al.*, "The US sulphur dioxide cap and trade programme and lessons for climate policy" http://voxeu.org/article/lessons-climate-policy-us-sulphur-dioxide-cap-and-trade-programme

Stern, Nicholas, "The Economics of Climate Change", *American Economic Review*, Papers and Proceedings, Richard T. Ely Lecture, January 4, 2008, http://ww.aeaweb.org/articles.php?doi=10.1257.aer.98.2.1

Sullivan, Dan, "Why Pittsburgh Real Estate Never Crashes," http://savingcommunities.org/places/us/pa/al/pgh/nevercrashes.html#t33

Tholstrup, Knud, "Economic Liberalism" https://hgarchives.files.wordpress.com/2017/05/tholstrup-economic-liberalism-feb-1973.pdf

Tideman, Nicolaus and Plassmann, Florenz, "Accurate Valuation in the Absence of Markets", *Public Finance Review*, Vol. 36 No. 3, May, 20087, pp. 334-358

Tideman, Nicolaus, Integrating Land Value Taxation with the Internalization of Spatial Externalities, *Land Economics*, Vol. 66, #3, August 1990

United Nations Division for Ocean Affairs and Law of the Sea, "United Nations Convention on the Law of the Sea" http://www.un.org/depts/los/convention_agreements/convention_overview_convention.htm

United Nations Office for Outer Space Affairs, "Space Law Treaties and Principles" http://www.unoosa.org/oosa/en/ourwork/spacelaw/treaties.html

United States Environmental Protection Agency, *U.S. Greenhouse Gas Inventory Report: 1990-2014*, https://www.epa.gov/ghgemissions/us-greenhouse-gas-inventory-report-1990-2014

Vickrey, William, Auerbach, Alan and Minarik, Joseph, "Federal Tax Policy for the 1990s", American Economic Association, 1992 Annual Papers and Proceedings, pp. 257-73

Warnock, John W., *Oil and Gas Royalties, Corporate Profits, and the Disregarded Public,* Parkland Institute and Canadian Centre for Policy Alternatives - Saskatchewan Office, 2006

Williams, Percy, "The Pittsburgh Graded Tax Plan," three articles published in *The American Journal of Economics and Sociology,* 1962-63, reprinted at http://savingcommunities.org/docs/williams.percy/gradedtax.html#g139

Contributors

Ted Gwartney.

Ted Gwartney, M. A. I., organized and was the Assessment Commissioner and Chief Executive Officer of the British Columbia Assessment Authority with 27 district offices and 765 employees. He implemented the annual Province-wide revaluation of the 1,500,000 land parcels, currently valued at over one half trillion dollars. He retired as the Assessor of Greenwich, Connecticut in 2012. Formerly he was the City Assessor of Bridgeport, Connecticut; Southfield, Michigan; Hartford, Connecticut; and the Deputy County Assessor of Sacramento, California.

Ted has been associated with the Robert Schalkenbach Foundation since 1970. He served as the Executive Director from 1996 to 2000 and was President from 2015 to 2017. He is the President, of the American Journal of Economics and Sociology and is Vice-President, of the Council of Georgist Organizations. He holds a MAI Professional Designation, from the Appraisal Institute. He was a Professor, in the Department of Law, on Real Estate Appraisal, at Baruch College, New York. He consults with Governments on finance and legal cases.

Dave Wetzel

Dave is a green socialist who since the age of 14 has campaigned for annual Land Value Tax and radical transport policies promoting walking, cycling and public transport. From bus conductor to Chair of London Buses; from active trade unionist at Heathrow airport to Vice-Chair of Transport for London, from an elected local Councillor at 21 to Chair of the Greater London Council's Transport Committee, from a Co-op Political Organiser to the Leader of a London Borough; from a factory worker to international speaker on land reform - Dave has stayed true to his principles and without any university training has spent a lifetime studying how to improve mankind's lot on this fragile planet.

Josh Vincent

Joshua Vincent is the Executive Director of the Center for the Study of Economics, based in Philadelphia Pennsylvania. His work concentration is project oriented; helping cities (or any other taxing jurisdiction) adopt land value taxation, if appropriate. Josh writes letters, blogs, and speaks to groups or elected officials to raise awareness and educate people about LVT, and how it can reduce and eventually eliminate taxation on work and capital investment. After education, CSE also conducts revenue impact studies jurisdictions to determine if LVT is politically possible, and would target what our knowledge to be serious problems facing municipalities. Josh also assists municipalities in setting their land value tax rates, engaging in follow-up, and expanding reliance on land values to provide information for researchers in other disciplines, as well as helping people directly. Josh's dream is to eliminate sales, income, business, and building taxes at the city or state level.

Josh also appears that many professional conclaves across the country to answer the most basic in queries about LVT and to highlight existing problems with current tax policy options. He is a smitten husband, prodigious gardener and slams a mean electric bass with his band, the Lumpen Proles.

Gary Flomenhoft

Gary Flomenhoft is an International Post-Graduate (IPRS) and University of Queensland Centennial Scholar and PhD Candidate at Centre for Social Responsibility in Mining. His research area is the economic value of common wealth and governance of Sovereign Wealth Funds.

Gary was a faculty member for 11 years in Community and International Development and Natural Resources at the University of Vermont. He conducted many development projects in The Commonwealth of Dominica, St. Lucia, and Belize with students and local partners. He also originated and coordinated the Green Building Design Program at UVM.

He had a secondary appointment as a Research Associate and Fellow at the Gund Institute for Ecological Economics. His primary research was in public finance for the state of Vermont including green/environmental taxes, common wealth and common assets, subsidy reform, and public banking. He directed the grant funded Green Tax and Common Assets project at the Gund Institute for seven years, where he originated the Vermont Common Assets Trust Fund (VCAT) bill, which was submitted to the legislature twice.

Mason Gaffney

Mason Gaffney has been Professor of Economics at U.C. Riverside, 1976-2013, retiring at age 89. He is a leading national voice on urban, land, resource and public finance economics, with a lifetime of publications and accomplishments. He is the author of (with Fred Harrison) The Corruption of Economics (1994), After the Crash: Designing a Depression-Free Economy (2009), The Mason Gaffney Reader (2010) and numerous papers, which are collected at www.masongaffney.org.

He had founded the British Columbia Inst. for Ec. Policy Analysis, and advised the Hon. Minister of Lands and Forests to hire Ted Gwartney to reorganize, permanently, the Province-wide Property Assessment Service and lead the local Assessors in raising assessed values of land relative to improvements.

He was Prof. of Economics at the University of Wisconsin-Milwaukee, where he teamed with Prof. Art Becker, a native there, to draw a map of City land values and use it to publicize errors in the work of the City Assessor. Becker and Gaffney also teamed to found and sustain TRED (Committee on Taxation, Resources, and Economic Development), engaging many leading economists in reviving the ideas of Henry George.

At the Univ. of Oregon, he got interested in timber management. To answer his questions about timber management he had to teach himself the mathematics of finance, something omitted from his earlier Ph.D. preparations at U.C. Berkeley. The resulting monograph, "Concepts of Financal Maturity of Timber." jumped him from being "Just another nice boy with good grades" to being a prospective starlet in the then-new world of mathematical economics – the first of several strokes of blind luck that characterize survival in academe.

Alanna Hartzok

Alanna Hartzok has spent her career campaigning for and teaching about economic justice via the Georgist paradigm. She was the Democratic (2014) and Green Party (2001) candidate for Congress in Pennsylvania's 9th District. She received the Radical Middle Book Award for her book *The Earth Belongs to Everyone*. She serves as International Liaison for the Robert Schalkenbach Foundation and as the Administrative Director for The International Union for Land Value Taxation. Co-founder, Earth Rights Institute. Recipient of International Earth Day Award; United Nations non-governmental organization representative.

Lindy Davies

Lindy Davies is one of the era's foremost Georgist Educators. He was introduced to Georgist political economy in 1983 by the indefaguitable Mike Curtis, who brought out whiteboards to teach his arboreal crew during lunch hours. He thought the ideas sounded too good to be true, but has yet to find the flaw.

He has served as the Program Director of the Henry George Instutute, and Editor/Designer of the *Georgist Journal* since 1995. He created the first online distance-learning program for the HGI, and in 2011-12 successfully earned college-credit recommendation for its "Principles of Political Economy" courses.

He created the abridged edition of Henry George's *The Science of Political Economy* in 2006, and is the author of *The Alodia Scrapbook: Creating a New Paradigm* (2003) in which online respondents were invited to help create a fictional Georgist nation in West Africa, and of the novel *The Sassafras Crossing (2016)*. He is a dad, a convinced Quaker, and a compulsive do-it-yourselfer.

Index

A

I

income capitalization approach,
 cannot yield accurate assessment on underused land 34
income taxes
 adoption of payroll taxes in
  1940s 104
 capacity to socialize rent 102
 importance of to Georgist
  policy 108
 nominally do not allow depreciation of land 106
 on forests 82
 transformed into tax on workers 104
Institutional Economics, by John R.
 Commons 105
international law of the sea 144
international sovereignty 124
Investment Tax Credit, repealed in
 1986 105

J

Johnson, Boris 54
Jubilee Line Extension 53
Justice Party, Denmark 71

K

Khan, Sadiq 56
Knight, Frank 106

L

land
 economic role thought to be
  insignificant 9, 11, 21
 economic sense of, defined 21
 essential to every form of production 127
 has market value for three
  reasons 23
 main source of "capital gains" 102

the commons 47
volatile element in real estate
 market 10
land assessment
 cost approach 34
 ground rent capitalization 44
 income capitalization approach
  34
 land residual technique 35
 must be subject to public examination 32
 procedures for 30–32
 role of local people's percep-
  tions in 31
 sales adjustment grids 39
 sales comparison approach 34
 standard units of measure 36
 subdivision development 45

Land Residual Technique 35, 41,
 43
land revenue systems, can be created even if valuation not
 currently in place 31
land use, inefficient under conventional land systems 25
land value
 and national sovereignty 125
 constrained by societal restrictions 28
 created by community 23
 decreased by poor maintenance
  of infrastructure 48
 increased by demand, not cost
  107
 increased by transport facilities 48
 increases from transport improvements can take years
  to appear 53
 often allocated to buildings,
  and depreciated 107

The Henry George Institute
www.henrygeorge.org

Since its founding in 1971, the Henry George Institute has led the movement to provide a high-quality, multi-purpose curriculum to promulgate the fundamentals of political economy and the insights articulated by Henry George in *Progress and Poverty* and other works. Thousands have studied with us, describing our courses as mind-opening experiences.

Correspondence students come from dozens of countries and all walks of life, making real our motto, **"You CAN Understand Economics!"** In the mid 1990s, when the Web was Young, we established our first online courses. In 2012, after a thorough review and beef-up of our program, we secured a college transfer credit recommendation from the National College Credit Recommendation Service. HGI students can receive an official transcript from Excelsior College, an accredited college in New York, which is recommended for three semester-hours of credit.

Really though, it's WAY more than just credit! It's what every thinking person needs to know about society and wealth. The first part of our study, *Understanding Economics*, is online, self-paced, and *entirely free!*

"I truly cannot overestimate the importance this course had for me. It made things more clear to me in a field I had little hope of understanding, and it has encouraged me to continue pursuing an interest in economics." — N. A., Israel

The course was a thorough, clear, and edifying experience that I can't recommend highly enough. Whereas the text of *Progress and Poverty* shall remain timeless, the supplementary material deserves special praise for its references to modern dilemmas and experiences — K. H., Washington

Robert Schalkenbach Foundation
PUBLISHER OF HENRY GEORGE AND RELATED WORKS – ADVOCATE FOR ECONOMIC JUSTICE

Robert Schalkenbach
(1856-1924)

Robert Schalkenbach Foundation

RSF was organized in 1925 as a private operating foundation to promote public awareness of the social philosophy and economic reforms advocated by Henry George. To this end, RSF conducts research, holds seminars, and publishes and distributes articles and books, including *Progress and Poverty* (1879), George's best-selling original classic, as well as a new abridgement using the language of the 21st century. These and other works can be accessed from our online library: *www.schalkenbach.org/on-line-library/works-by-henry-george/* We also offer hard copy books for purchase from our online bookstore: *www.schalkenbach.org/shop/*

Henry George
(1839-1897)

Henry George (September 2, 1839 – October 29, 1897)
was an American writer, political economist, and social reformer. He was also the most influential proponent of replacing all taxes with a *Land Value Tax*, which became known around the world as the *Single Tax*. The *Georgist* philosophy and economic analysis begins with the premise that Land (all natural resources and urban sites), provided by nature and made valuable by society, belongs equally to all humanity, and that each person owns the products of his or her own Labor, mental and physical, that is necessarily applied to Land. George's masterpiece, *Progress and Poverty* (1879), offers a reform program as the remedy for the poverty and economic depressions caused by land monopoly and speculation.

Robert Schalkenbach Foundation
211 East 43rd St. #400, New York, NY 10017 USA

Tel: 212-683-6424   Fax: 212-683-6454   Toll-free: 800-269-9555
www.schalkenbach.org   books@schalkenbach.org   info@schalkenbach.org

www.earthsharing.org

 EARTH SHARING.org

Earth Sharing is a non-partisan initiative of Robert Schalkenbach Foundation to promote the ideals of Henry George. We invite people to think and ask questions. What are the institutional causes of poverty? What can we do as a society to incentivize environmentally sustainable behavior? Why does it matter? What can I personally do to improve the situation?

95069752R00098

Made in the USA
Columbia, SC
06 May 2018